LEARN KOTLIN

From Fundamentals to Practical Applications

2024 Edition

Diego Rodrigues

LEARN KOTLIN
From Fundamentals to Practical Applications

2024 Edition
Author: Diego Rodrigues

Important Note

The codes and scripts presented in this book aim to illustrate the concepts discussed in the chapters, serving as practical examples. These examples were developed in custom, controlled environments, and therefore there is no guarantee that they will work fully in all scenarios. It is essential to check the configurations and customizations of the environment where they will be applied to ensure their proper functioning. We thank you for your understanding.

GREETINGS, DEAR READER!

It is with great enthusiasm that I welcome you on this journey of learning about Kotlin, a modern, concise and powerful language. Your decision to invest in improving your skills is a clear demonstration of your commitment to personal and professional development. I want to make sure this book is more than just a technical manual: it will be your compass for exploring the vast possibilities that Kotlin offers.

Technology rewards those who seek to understand its nuances and apply them creatively. However, it also requires constant dedication to keep up with its evolution. It was with this in mind that we created this book, designed as a practical technical guide, ideal for those who want to learn quickly, efficiently and in depth.

"Learn Kotlin" is designed to provide a comprehensive and applied understanding of this language, from its fundamentals to its most advanced capabilities. The progressive structure and in-depth content will allow you to not only master the essential concepts but also apply them directly to real-world projects, whether they are aimed at Android development, robust backends, or cross-platform solutions.

We live in a world where being up to date is more than a differentiator — it's a necessity. The knowledge acquired here will serve as a basis for you to stand out in a competitive and constantly changing scenario. This book has been carefully developed to ensure that each chapter enriches your skills and broadens your horizons.

Prepare for a learning experience that will transform the way you program and solve problems. This is the beginning of an exciting journey towards excellence in development with Kotlin. Welcome aboard this adventure into the future of programming.

Let's start together!

ABOUT THE AUTHOR

www.linkedin.com/in/diegoexpertai

Best-Selling Author, Diego Rodrigues is an International Consultant and Writer specializing in Market Intelligence, Technology and Innovation. With 42 international certifications from institutions such as IBM, Google, Microsoft, AWS, Cisco, and Boston University, Ec-Council, Palo Alto and META.

Rodrigues is an expert in Artificial Intelligence, Machine Learning, Data Science, Big Data, Blockchain, Connectivity Technologies, Ethical Hacking and Threat Intelligence.

Since 2003, Rodrigues has developed more than 200 projects for important brands in Brazil, USA and Mexico. In 2024, he consolidates himself as one of the largest new generation authors of technical books in the world, with more than 180 titles published in six languages.

BOOK PRESENTATION

Welcome to Kotlin: The Language of the Future

We live in an era where mastering the right development tools can transform ideas into tangible, efficient realities. If you're holding this book — or, right now, trying out this free preview — congratulations! You are one step away from equipping yourself with one of the most powerful and flexible resources in the world of programming: the Kotlin language.

Why Kotlin?

Kotlin is a modern, elegant and highly productive language that was designed to solve real problems faced by developers in a world where mobile applications, robust backends and cross-platform solutions are essential. Created by JetBrains, Kotlin quickly became the language of choice for Android development and gained recognition as a powerful alternative for backend and cross-platform applications.

If you've worked with languages like Java, Python, or JavaScript, you'll realize that Kotlin combines the best of all worlds: the typesafety and reliability of Java, the syntactical simplicity of Python, and the flexibility of JavaScript. Furthermore, it is completely interoperable with Java, allowing you to integrate existing projects without rewriting everything from scratch.

The goal of this book is simple: to be the definitive guide for your journey with Kotlin, helping you master everything from the fundamentals to the most advanced and practical applications.

Target Audience

This book was created with a wide audience in mind, from

beginners who have never programmed before to experienced developers who want to explore Kotlin for their modern needs. It is ideal for:

- **Students and beginners** who are learning their first programming language.
- **Technology professionals** who want to master Android or backend development with Kotlin.
- **Java Developers** who want to migrate or complement their skills with Kotlin.
- **Technology enthusiasts** interested in exploring functional programming and cross-platform development.

Our commitment is to offer a didactic and progressive approach, with clear explanations, practical examples and exercises that consolidate learning.

How This Book Is Structured

To ensure you have a complete and enriching experience, we have divided the content into 25 carefully crafted chapters. Each chapter is designed to build on the concepts of the previous one, ensuring continuous and cumulative learning. Here's a brief overview of what you'll find:

- **Chapters 1 to 3:** We explore the basics, such as the history of Kotlin, installing the necessary tools, and the structure of a program. Even if you've never written a line of code, these chapters will prepare you.
- **Chapters 4 to 6:** Let's delve into the basics of programming, including flow control, functions, and collection manipulation. These are the foundations for creating robust applications.
- **Chapters 7 to 9:** We introduce advanced object-oriented programming concepts such as inheritance, interfaces and abstractions, making your code more modular and reusable.
- **Chapters 10 to 12:** We focus on string manipulation,

file operations and exception handling. These topics are essential for creating complete and resilient applications.

- **Chapters 13 to 15:** We get into more sophisticated concepts like functional, object-oriented, and asynchronous programming. Here, you will begin to understand why Kotlin is so powerful.
- **Chapters 16 to 22:** We cover practical applications, including API integration, data persistence, automated testing, and cross-platform development. You will learn how to create real-world applications that are scalable and efficient.
- **Chapters 23 to 25:** We finish with best practices, code patterns, and a glimpse into the future of Kotlin. This is the point where you reflect on the impact of everything you have learned and prepare to continue your journey.

What Makes This Book Unique?

1. **Practical Approach:** This is not just a theory book. Each chapter includes real examples, practical exercises and tips for solving everyday problems in software development.
2. **Structured Progression:** We start from the basics and move on to complex topics, leaving no gaps in learning.
3. **Comprehensive Coverage:** From Android development to backend, from Kotlin Multiplatform to modern functional programming practices, this book covers every aspect you need to master to be a well-rounded Kotlin developer.
4. **Clear and Concise Style:** We know your time is valuable. This book was written to convey information clearly and bluntly.

Why Should You Move Forward?

Learning Kotlin is not just a technical decision; It's an investment in your future. Companies across the world are adopting Kotlin for its efficiency and simplicity. Its application goes far beyond Android development, covering backend, corporate systems and even multiplatform projects that share code between Android, iOS and more.

When you master Kotlin, you won't just be learning a language; You will be acquiring a powerful tool to transform your career and expand your creative possibilities.

Your Journey Starts Here

I invite you to join me on this exciting journey. With each chapter, you'll discover new ways to think, create, and solve problems with Kotlin. Whether you're a curious beginner or a seasoned pro looking to refresh, this book is your ally in exploring Kotlin's limitless potential.

So what are you waiting for? Take the next step, dive into the first chapter and see how Kotlin can transform the way you program. The future of development is here, and it starts now.

Let's get started!?

CHAPTER 1: INTRODUCTION TO KOTLIN

History and Evolution of Language

Kotlin is a modern programming language designed by JetBrains, the same company responsible for developing popular tools like IntelliJ IDEA. Its initial release took place in 2011, and its objective was to provide a more concise and expressive alternative to Java, especially for the development of Android and backend applications.

The evolution of Kotlin has been marked by steady growth, driven by its interoperability with Java and increasing adoption by developers and companies around the world. In 2017, Kotlin was officially recognized as a supported language for Android development by Google, further consolidating its position in the technology market.

Today, Kotlin is widely used not only in Android development, but also in backend, cross-platform applications, and even in data science. Its modern design and innovative functionalities make it a preferred choice for projects that require high productivity and code quality.

Why Kotlin Was Created and Its Advantages

Kotlin was developed to overcome some of the limitations of Java and other programming languages while maintaining an accessible learning curve for both experienced and beginner programmers. Below are some of the reasons for its creation and advantages that make it stand out in the current scenario:

1. Concise and Clear Syntax

Kotlin significantly reduces the amount of code needed to perform common tasks. For example, unlike Java, you don't need to write extensive blocks of code to implement default getters, setters, or initializations.

kotlin

```
// Kotlin
data class User(val name: String, val age: Int)
```

```
// Java (equivalent)
public class User {
    private String name;
    private int age;

    public User(String name, int age) {
        this.name = name;
        this.age = age;
    }

    public String getName() {
        return name;
    }

    public int getAge() {
        return age;
    }
}
```

2. Interoperability with Java

Kotlin is fully compatible with Java, allowing existing projects to use both languages side by side. This makes it easier to migrate large legacy systems and reuse existing Java libraries.

3. Security Against NullPointerException

The famous "NullPointerException" is one of the most common errors in languages like Java. Kotlin addresses this problem by handling null values directly at the type level.

kotlin

```kotlin
// Null safety example
fun printLength(str: String?) {
    println(str?.length ?: "String is null")
}
```

In this example, the operator ?. checks whether the variable is null before accessing its property, while the operator ?: provides a default value if the variable is null.

4. Native Functional Programming Support

Kotlin combines object-oriented and functional programming concepts, allowing you to enjoy the best of both worlds. Features like lambdas, high-order functions, and immutable collections make data manipulation more elegant and efficient.

Kotlin Ecosystem

Kotlin is incredibly versatile, being widely adopted in many areas of development. Here are the main components of its ecosystem:

1. Android

The main application of Kotlin is in Android development. Thanks to official support from Google, Kotlin has become the preferred language for creating mobile applications. Its libraries, such as Kotlin Coroutines and Android KTX, make it easy to develop well-structured, responsive applications.

kotlin

```kotlin
// Basic Android activity example
class MainActivity : AppCompatActivity() {
    override fun onCreate(savedInstanceState: Bundle?) {
        super.onCreate(savedInstanceState)
        setContentView(R.layout.activity_main)

        findViewById<Button>(R.id.button).setOnClickListener {
```

```
        Toast.makeText(this, "Hello, Kotlin!",
Toast.LENGTH_SHORT).show()
      }
   }
}
```

The code above exemplifies how to configure a button to display a "toast" message in an Android application using Kotlin.

2. Backend

Kotlin is also widely used in backend development, thanks to frameworks like Ktor, Spring, and Micronaut. Its modern syntax and coroutine support make it simple to create scalable and efficient servers.

kotlin

```
// Exemplo básico de servidor com Which
fun main() {
   embeddedServer(Netty, port = 8080) {
      routing {
         get("/") {
            call.respondText("Hello, Backend with Kotlin!")
         }
      }
   }.start(wait = true)
}
```

In this example, we create a simple web server with Ktor, which responds with a message when accessing the root route.

3. Cross-platform

Kotlin Multiplatform allows you to share business logic between different platforms, such as Android, iOS, and even the web. This feature is ideal for companies that want to reduce costs and development time by reusing code across multiple projects.

kotlin

```kotlin
// Basic example of shared code
expect fun platformName(): String

fun createMessage(): String {
    return "Hello from ${platformName()}"
}
```

The function expect allows you to define specific implementations for each platform, while shared logic resides in the same code.

Kotlin is more than just a language; is a robust and modern tool that empowers developers to create high-quality applications across multiple platforms. Once you master Kotlin, you'll be ready to face the challenges of modern development with efficiency and confidence. In the next chapters, we will explore everything from setting up the development environment to advanced applications, ensuring you make the most of the capabilities of this powerful language.

CHAPTER 2: CONFIGURING THE DEVELOPMENT ENVIRONMENT

Development with Kotlin requires a correctly configured environment so that the coding experience is fluid and efficient. This chapter covers installing the necessary tools, creating a working Kotlin project, and using additional tools that increase development productivity.

Installing IntelliJ IDEA

IntelliJ IDEA, created by JetBrains, is the recommended integrated development environment (IDE) for working with Kotlin. It offers full language support, including features such as syntax highlighting, autocompletion, debugging, and integration with version control tools.

1. Visit the official IntelliJ IDEA website at https://www.jetbrains.com/idea.
2. Download the desired version. The Community version is free and sufficient for basic and intermediate Kotlin projects. The paid Ultimate version is more suitable for advanced corporate projects.
3. After downloading, run the installer and follow the instructions. During installation, check the options to create shortcuts and associate files .kt ao IntelliJ IDEA
4. Open IntelliJ IDEA and configure initial options such as the interface theme and plugins. Make sure the Kotlin plugin is activated.

Installing Android Studio

For developing Android apps with Kotlin, Android Studio is the official tool and offers native integration with Kotlin.

1. Access https://developer.android.com/studio and download the latest version of Android Studio.
2. Run the installer and follow the instructions. During installation, configure the Android SDK and download the necessary packages for emulators and Kotlin support.
3. After installation, open Android Studio and configure the emulator if you want to test your applications without using a physical device.

Creating your First Kotlin Project

With the environment configured, you can create a project to explore Kotlin. To do this, we will use IntelliJ IDEA as an example.

1. Open IntelliJ IDEA and click "New Project" on the home screen.
2. Select "Kotlin" from the project types menu. Choose "Kotlin/JVM" to create a project that uses the Java virtual machine (JVM).
3. Define the project name and the directory where it will be saved.
4. Configure the SDK. If you don't already have an SDK installed, click "Add SDK" and choose the option to install the latest JDK.
5. After creating the project, IntelliJ IDEA generates a basic directory structure.

Create a new Kotlin file with the name Main.kt inside the directory src. In the file, add the following code:

kotlin

```kotlin
fun main() {
    println("Hello, Kotlin!")
}
```

This program defines the main function, which is the entry point of Kotlin. The function println displays the specified text in the console.

Run the program by clicking the "Run" icon next to the function main. The console will display the message "Hello, Kotlin!".

Setting up a Kotlin Project in Android Studio

Android Studio also supports Kotlin since project creation. To set up an Android project with Kotlin:

1. Open Android Studio and click "Start a new Android Studio project".
2. Choose a home screen template, such as "Empty Activity".
3. Set the application name, save location, and language to Kotlin. Configure the minimum API as per your project requirements.
4. Once finished, Android Studio creates an Android project with Kotlin support enabled.

The main project file is MainActivity.kt. It already contains some basic code:

kotlin

```kotlin
class MainActivity : AppCompatActivity() {
    override fun onCreate(savedInstanceState: Bundle?) {
        super.onCreate(savedInstanceState)
        setContentView(R.layout.activity_main)
    }
}
```

This class inherits from AppCompatActivity, which is the basis for creating screens on Android. The method onCreate configures the activity layout, using the XML file located in res/layout/activity_main.xml. To add a button and handle events, modify the layout and code as follows:

In the archive activity_main.xml, enter:

xml

```
<Button
    android:id="@+id/button"
    android:layout_width="wrap_content"
    android:layout_height="wrap_content"
    android:text="Click Me"
    android:layout_gravity="center" />
```

In the archive MainActivity.kt, add logic for the button:

kotlin

```
override fun onCreate(savedInstanceState: Bundle?) {
    super.onCreate(savedInstanceState)
    setContentView(R.layout.activity_main)

    val button = findViewById<Button>(R.id.button)
    button.setOnClickListener {
        Toast.makeText(this, "Button clicked!",
Toast.LENGTH_SHORT).show()
    }
}
```

This code finds the button in the layout by its ID and sets up a click listener to display a message when pressed.

Additional Tools and Tips for Productivity

Several complementary tools help increase productivity when developing with Kotlin.

Dependency Management with Gradle

Gradle is the standard tool for managing dependencies in Kotlin projects. The file build.gradle controls which external libraries are used.

To add a dependency, insert the library into the file build.gradle:

gradle

```
dependencies {
    implementation("org.jetbrains.kotlin:kotlin-stdlib:1.8.0")
}
```

After editing the file, synchronize the project so that Gradle can download and configure the libraries.

Using IntelliJ IDEA Plugins

IntelliJ IDEA allows you to install plugins to improve the development experience. Some recommended plugins include:

- **Kotlin Code Style**: To maintain a consistent pattern in the code.
- **Key Promoter X**: To learn keyboard shortcuts and improve coding speed.
- **Git Integration**: For version control directly in the IDE.

Tips to Increase Productivity

- Use keyboard shortcuts for common actions. For example, Ctrl+Shift+F10 runs the current program.
- Enable "Live Templates" to create shortcuts of frequent code snippets.
- Enable "Code With Me" in IntelliJ IDEA for real-time remote collaboration.

Setting up the environment correctly and exploring additional tools makes developing with Kotlin more efficient and enjoyable. This chapter provides the first steps so you can start writing programs and creating applications with confidence.

CHAPTER 3: BASIC SYNTAX AND PROGRAM STRUCTURE

The Kotlin language is designed to be expressive, concise, and safe. Mastering basic syntax is critical to building efficient programs and understanding best practices for developing clean, robust code.

Declaring Variables: our and val

In Kotlin, variables are declared with the keywords our and val.

- our is used to declare mutable variables, i.e., whose value can be changed during program execution.
- val is used to declare immutable variables, that is, those whose value cannot be changed after initialization.

kotlin

```
var mutableVariable = 10
val immutableVariable = 20
```

In the code above, the variable mutableVariable can be changed later, but immutableVariable will remain at the value assigned at the time of declaration.

Change the value of a variable declared with our:

kotlin

```
mutableVariable = 15
```

Attempting to change the value of a variable declared with val will result in compilation error. This ensures greater security and makes it easier to track immutable states in the program.

The use of val is encouraged whenever possible, as it reduces the risk of accidental modifications and helps create more predictable code.

Type Inference and Data Types in Kotlin

Kotlin has a strong type system and supports type inference. This means that you can, in most cases, omit the explicit type declaration, as the compiler will automatically deduce the variable's type based on the assigned value.

Type Inference

Type inference is applied when the variable is initialized at declaration time.

kotlin

```
val number = 42 // Inferred type as Int
val text = "Hello, Kotlin!" // Type inferred as String
```

Although type inference is convenient, you can explicitly declare the type if necessary:

kotlin

```
val number: Int = 42
val text: String = "Hello, Kotlin!"
```

Declaring the type explicitly can be useful for clarity or when the type is not immediately evident.

Data Types

Kotlin supports multiple data types such as numbers, strings, booleans, and lists.

Numbers

Numeric data types include Int, Double, Float, Long, Short and Byte.

kotlin

```
val intNumber: Int = 100
val doubleNumber: Double = 3.14
val floatNumber: Float = 2.5F
val longNumber: Long = 100000L
val shortNumber: Short = 10
val byteNumber: Byte = 1
```

Strings

Strings are used to store text and can be declared in double quotes. Kotlin also supports multiline strings, delimited by three double quotes.

kotlin

```
val singleLine = "Hello, Kotlin!"
val multiLine = """
    This is a
    multi-line string.
"""
```

It is possible to insert variables or expressions within strings using interpolation:

kotlin

```
val name = "Kotlin"
val greeting = "Hello, $name!" // "Hello, Kotlin!"
```

Booleanos

Boolean variables store values true or false.

kotlin

```
val isKotlinFun: Boolean = true
val isJavaOld: Boolean = false
```

Lists and Maps

Kotlin supports lists and maps as common data structures. Lists can be mutable (MutableList) or immutable (List).

kotlin

```kotlin
val immutableList = listOf(1, 2, 3)
val mutableList = mutableListOf(1, 2, 3)
mutableList.add(4)

val immutableMap = mapOf("key1" to "value1", "key2" to
"value2")
val mutableMap = mutableMapOf("key1" to "value1")
mutableMap["key2"] = "value2"
```

Basic Structure of a Program

A Kotlin program starts by defining a main function called main, which is the entry point of the program.

kotlin

```kotlin
fun main() {
    println("Hello, World!")
}
```

In this program, the function main uses println to display a message on the console. The basic structure of a Kotlin program includes functions, variable declarations, and expressions.

Functions

Functions in Kotlin are defined with the keyword fun, followed by the function name, parameters, and body.

kotlin

```kotlin
fun addNumbers(a: Int, b: Int): Int {
    return a + b
```

```
}
```

The above function takes two integers as parameters and returns their sum. Kotlin also supports single expression functions, which omit the keyword return and the keys.

kotlin

```
fun multiplyNumbers(a: Int, b: Int) = a * b
```

Conditionals

Kotlin supports conditional structures such as if-else. In many cases, the if can be used as an expression that returns a value.

kotlin

```
fun max(a: Int, b: Int): Int {
    return if (a > b) a else b
}
```

In the example, the if returns the largest value between a and b.

Control Structures

Kotlin includes control structures like when, which is more expressive than a switch traditional.

kotlin

```
fun describeNumber(number: Int): String {
    return when (number) {
        0 -> "Zero"
        1 -> "One"
        in 2..10 -> "Between two and ten"
        else -> "Other"
    }
}
```

In the code above, the function returns a description based on the value of the variable number.

Repeating Loops

Kotlin supports loops like for, while and do-while.

kotlin

```kotlin
fun printNumbers() {
    for (i in 1..5) {
        println(i)
    }
}
```

The noose for cycles through the numbers 1 to 5 and prints each number.

Classes and Objects

Kotlin is an object-oriented language. A class can be defined with the keyword class.

kotlin

```kotlin
class Person(val name: String, var age: Int)

fun main() {
    val person = Person("Alice", 25)
    println("${person.name} is ${person.age} years old.")
}
```

The class Person has a primary constructor that initializes the attributes name and age. When instantiating the class, values are passed as arguments.

Best Practices

- Use val whenever possible to create immutable variables, reducing the risk of errors.
- Prefer type inference to improve code readability, but explicitly declare types in cases where the intent may be

unclear.

- Use interpolated strings to compose messages or create dynamic formats.
- Break complex functions into several smaller, simpler functions.
- Avoid using global variables. Prefer passing information as parameters to functions.
- Document code using clear comments, but avoid redundant comments that explain something obvious.

Understanding basic syntax and program structure is essential for effective Kotlin development. By applying good practices, it is possible to create clear, efficient and easy-to-maintain applications.

CHAPTER 4: FLOW CONTROL

Flow control is essential for developing dynamic and interactive programs. It allows decisions to be made, structures to be repeated, and actions to be taken based on specific conditions. Kotlin offers several tools for flow control, including conditionals, repetition structures, and alternative expressions.

Conditionals: if, else and when

Conditional if

The structure if is used to make decisions based on conditions. In Kotlin, it can be used as a statement or an expression.

As instruction

An instruction if executes a block of code based on the evaluation of a condition.

kotlin

```kotlin
fun checkEven(number: Int) {
    if (number % 2 == 0) {
        println("$number is even")
    }
}
```

If the condition number % 2 == 0 is true, the code inside the block will be executed.

As an expression

The structure if can return values.

kotlin

```kotlin
fun max(a: Int, b: Int): Int {
    return if (a > b) a else b
}
```

In the code above, the structure if evaluates which number is greater and returns the result. This eliminates the need to create temporary variables or use redundant structures.

Conditional else

The clause else complements the instruction if, providing an alternative path when the evaluated condition is false.

kotlin

```kotlin
fun checkSign(number: Int) {
    if (number > 0) {
        println("Positive")
    } else {
        println("Negative or Zero")
    }
}
```

When number is greater than zero, the message "Positive" will be displayed. Otherwise, "Negative or Zero" will be shown.

Conditional if-else if

When several conditions need to be checked, the if-else if is used.

kotlin

```kotlin
fun gradeEvaluation(score: Int): String {
    return if (score >= 90) {
        "Excellent"
    } else if (score >= 75) {
        "Good"
    } else if (score >= 50) {
        "Pass"
```

```
    } else {
        "Fail"
    }
}
```

The code evaluates the score and returns a string representing the corresponding performance.

Conditional when

THE when is a powerful structure that replaces the switch traditional found in other languages. It allows you to evaluate multiple conditions with more clarity and less repetitive code.

With fixed values
kotlin

```
fun getDayType(day: String): String {
    return when (day) {
        "Saturday", "Sunday" -> "Weekend"
        "Monday", "Tuesday", "Wednesday", "Thursday", "Friday" ->
"Weekday"
        else -> "Invalid day"
    }
}
```

The code above evaluates the value of the variable day and returns the corresponding type.

With intervals
kotlin

```
fun evaluateNumber(number: Int): String {
    return when (number) {
        in 1..10 -> "Between 1 and 10"
        in 11..20 -> "Between 11 and 20"
        else -> "Out of range"
    }
}
```

The operator in checks if the value is within a range.

With types
kotlin

```
fun describe(value: Any): String {
    return when (value) {
        is Int -> "Integer"
        is String -> "String"
        is Boolean -> "Boolean"
        else -> "Unknown type"
    }
}
```

THE when can check the type of a variable, making it easier to dynamically use different types in a function.

Repetition Structures: for, while and do-while

Repetition structures are used to execute a block of code multiple times depending on conditions or iterations.

Link for

THE for is used to traverse collections, ranges, and sequences.

Iterating over intervals
kotlin

```
fun printNumbers() {
    for (i in 1..5) {
        println(i)
    }
}
```

The loop loops through the numbers 1 to 5, printing each one.

Controlling the pace
kotlin

```kotlin
fun printEvenNumbers() {
    for (i in 2..10 step 2) {
        println(i)
    }
}
```

The loop traverses the range 2 to 10, in increments of 2.

Iterating backwards

kotlin

```kotlin
fun printCountdown() {
    for (i in 10 downTo 1) {
        println(i)
    }
}
```

The keyword downTo allows you to iterate in descending order.

Iterating over collections

kotlin

```kotlin
fun printNames(names: List<String>) {
    for (name in names) {
        println(name)
    }
}
```

THE for loop through each element in the list names and prints its value.

Link while

THE while executes a block of code as long as a condition is true.

kotlin

```kotlin
fun countToTen() {
    where i = 1
```

```
    while (i <= 10) {
        println(i)
        i++
    }
}
```

The loop continues incrementing and printing the value of i as long as it is less than or equal to 10.

Link do-while

THE do-while is similar to while, but it guarantees that the block will be executed at least once.

kotlin

```
fun countDownFromTen() {
    where i = 10
    do {
        println(i)
        i--
    } while (i > 0)
}
```

Even if the condition is false from the beginning, the block will be executed once.

Using Expressions as Substitutes for Traditional Structures

Kotlin allows multiple control structures to be used as expressions, promoting more concise and functional code.

Replacing if-else

THE if-else can be used as an expression to return values directly.

kotlin

```
fun checkParity(number: Int): String {
    return if (number % 2 == 0) "Even" else "Odd"
```

}

The function returns "Even" or "Odd" depending on the parity of the number.

Replacing switch for the when

THE when is more flexible and can replace the switch, allowing complex conditions to be assessed.

kotlin

```kotlin
fun categorizeAge(age: Int): String {
    return when {
        age < 13 -> "Child"
        age in 13..19 -> "Teenager"
        age >= 20 -> "Adult"
        else -> "Invalid age"
    }
}
```

THE when evaluates multiple conditions without requiring a variable for direct comparison.

Flow control is the backbone of any programming language. With tools like if, else, when and loops, Kotlin offers a modern, expressive syntax that makes code more readable and efficient. The ability to use structures as expressions allows you to reduce redundancies and create clearer programs.

CHAPTER 5: ROLES AND SCOPES

Functions are fundamental elements in Kotlin and serve to encapsulate reusable blocks of code. The Kotlin language supports basic and advanced functions, including high-order functions, lambdas, inline functions, and scope extensions. Effective use of functions promotes modularity, readability, and code reuse.

Declaration and Use of Functions

Functions in Kotlin are declared with the keyword fun, followed by the function name, optional parameters, and return type.

kotlin

```kotlin
fun greetUser(name: String): String {
    return "Hello, $name!"
}
```

The function greetUser accepts a parameter of the type String and returns a personalized greeting. To use it, just call it with a valid argument.

kotlin

```kotlin
fun main() {
    val message = greetUser("Alice")
    println(message)
}
```

The code displays the message "Hello, Alice!".

Non-Return Functions

Functions that do not return values use the return type Unit, which can be omitted as it is implicit.

kotlin

```kotlin
fun printMessage(message: String) {
    println(message)
}
```

This function prints a message without returning any value.

Optional Parameters

Functions can have parameters with default values, making them optional in the call.

kotlin

```kotlin
fun greet(name: String = "Guest") {
    println("Welcome, $name!")
}
```

If no arguments are provided, the function uses the default value "Guest".

kotlin

```kotlin
greet() // Exibe "Welcome, Guest!"
greet("Bob") // Displays "Welcome, Bob!"
```

Functions with Expression Return

Single expression functions eliminate the need to use keywords return and {}.

kotlin

```kotlin
fun add(a: Int, b: Int) = a + b
```

This function returns the sum of a and b directly.

Function Overloading

Kotlin allows you to define multiple functions with the same name, as long as their signatures are different.

kotlin

```kotlin
fun display(value: Int) {
    println("Integer: $value")
}
fun display(value: String) {
    println("String: $value")
}
```

The correct function will be called based on the type of the argument provided.

Higher Order Functions

High-order functions are those that take other functions as parameters or return functions.

kotlin

```kotlin
fun calculate(a: Int, b: Int, operation: (Int, Int) -> Int): Int {
    return operation(a, b)
}
```

The function calculate receives two numbers and a function that defines the operation to be performed.

kotlin

```kotlin
val sum = calculate(5, 3) { x, y -> x + y }
println(sum) // Displays 8
```

The code applies the lambda function { x, y -> x + y } to calculate soma of 5 and 3.

Lambda Functions

Lambdas are anonymous functions defined with a compact

syntax.

kotlin

```
val multiply: (Int, Int) -> Int = { a, b -> a * b }
println(multiply(4, 5)) // Displays 20
```

No lambda { a, b -> a * b }, a and b are the parameters, and a * b is the body of the function.

Lambdas with a Single Parameter

If a lambda has only one parameter, it can be referenced directly by the keyword it.

kotlin

```
val square: (Int) -> Int = { it * it }
println(square(6)) // Displays 36
```

The keyword it represents the only parameter of the lambda.

Inline Functions

Inline functions allow lambdas to be embedded directly into code, reducing function call overhead.

kotlin

```
inline fun performOperation(a: Int, b: Int, operation: (Int, Int) -> Int): Int {
    return operation(a, b)
}
```

When an inline function is called, its body is replaced directly at the call location, improving performance in critical situations.

kotlin

```
val result = performOperation(10, 20) { x, y -> x + y }
println(result) // Displays 30
```

Role Scopes

The scope of a function defines where it can be accessed and executed.

Local Functions

Functions can be declared inside other functions for exclusive use within that context.

kotlin

```kotlin
fun calculateFactorial(n: Int): Int {
    fun factorial(x: Int): Int {
        return if (x == 1) 1 else x * factorial(x - 1)
    }
    return factorial(n)
}
```

The function factorial is only accessible within the function calculateFactorial.

Extension Functions

Extension functions allow you to add new behaviors to existing classes without modifying them directly.

kotlin

```kotlin
fun String.reverse(): String {
    return this.reversed()
}
```

This function adds rollback behavior to strings.

kotlin

```kotlin
val original = "Kotlin"
val reversed = original.reverse()
println(reversed) // Displays "niltoK"
```

Extension functions are useful for improving code readability and reusability.

Scope with Library Functions

Kotlin offers functions like let, run, apply, also and with to manipulate the scope of variables and objects in a functional way.

let

The function let is used to execute a block of code on an object and return the result.

kotlin

```
val result = "Kotlin".let {
    it.toUpperCase()
}
println(result) // Displays "KOTLIN"
```

run

The function run combines initialization and execution in a single block.

kotlin

```
val length = "Hello".run {
    this.length
}
println(length) // Exibe 5
```

apply

The function apply is used to configure objects, returning the object itself after executing the block.

kotlin

```
val person = Person().apply {
```

```
    name = "Alice"
    age = 30
}
println(person.name) // Displays "Alice"
```

also

The function also allows you to perform additional actions on an object without changing its return.

kotlin

```
val list = mutableListOf(1, 2, 3).also {
    it.add(4)
}
println(list) // Displays [1, 2, 3, 4]
```

with

The function with performs actions on an object as the main context.

kotlin

```
val fullName = with(Person()) {
    name = "Bob"
    "$name Smith"
}
println(fullName) // Displays "Bob Smith"
```

Kotlin offers a modern, functional approach to working with functions and scopes, promoting clean, efficient, and reusable code. Effective use of these tools is crucial to creating robust, well-structured applications.

CHAPTER 6: WORKING WITH COLLECTIONS

Kotlin offers a wide range of collections that make managing datasets easier. They are designed to be flexible and efficient, supporting common operations such as filtering, mapping, and grouping. Furthermore, Kotlin has the concept of sequences, which allows efficient processing of large volumes of data. Understanding how to work with lists, sets, and maps is essential for writing idiomatic and performative code.

Types of Collections: Lists, Sets and Maps

Collections in Kotlin can be immutable or mutable. Immutable ones do not allow modifications after creation, while mutable ones can be changed.

Lists

Lists are used to store elements in a specific order. They may contain duplicate items.

Immutable Lists

The function listOf creates an immutable list.

kotlin

```
val fruits = listOf("Apple", "Banana", "Cherry")
println(fruits[0]) // Displays "Apple"
```

List elements can be accessed using indexes, but cannot be changed.

Mutable Lists

The function mutableListOf creates a mutable list.

kotlin

```
val colors = mutableListOf("Red", "Green", "Blue")
colors.add("Yellow")
println(colors) // Exibe [Red, Green, Blue, Yellow]
```

The list can be modified by adding, removing or replacing elements.

Sets

Sets are collections of single, disordered elements.

Immutable Sets

The function setOf creates an immutable set.

kotlin

```
val uniqueNumbers = setOf(1, 2, 3, 3, 4)
println(uniqueNumbers) // Displays [1, 2, 3, 4]
```

Duplicate elements are automatically ignored.

Mutable Sets

The function mutableSetOf creates a mutable set.

kotlin

```
val numbers = mutableSetOf(1, 2, 3)
numbers.add(4)
println(numbers) // Exibe [1, 2, 3, 4]
```

The set can be modified, but it continues to guarantee the uniqueness of the elements.

Maps

Maps store key-value pairs. Each key must be unique, but values can be repeated.

Immutable Maps

The function mapOf creates an immutable map.

kotlin

```
val countryCodes = mapOf("US" to "United States", "BR" to "Brazil")
println(countryCodes["BR"]) // Exibe "Brazil"
```

The values can be accessed by the keys, but the map cannot be changed.

Mutable Maps

The function mutableMapOf creates a mutable map.

kotlin

```
val studentGrades = mutableMapOf("Alice" to 90, "Bob" to 85)
studentGrades["Charlie"] = 88
println(studentGrades) // Displays {Alice=90, Bob=85, Charlie=88}
```

You can add, update, or remove key-value pairs.

Common Operations

Kotlin simplifies operations such as filtering, mapping and grouping through collection extension methods.

Filtering

Filtering creates a new collection containing elements that meet a criteria.

kotlin

```
val numbers = listOf(1, 2, 3, 4, 5, 6)
val evenNumbers = numbers.filter { it % 2 == 0 }
println(evenNumbers) // Displays [2, 4, 6]
```

The method filter applies a condition to include only even

numbers.

Mapping

Mapping transforms each element of a collection by applying a function.

kotlin

```
val names = listOf("Alice", "Bob", "Charlie")
val nameLengths = names.map { it.length }
println(nameLengths) // Exibe [5, 3, 7]
```

The method map calculates the length of each name in the list.

Grouping

Grouping organizes elements into subcollections based on a key.

kotlin

```
val words = listOf("cat", "dog", "apple", "ant")
val groupedByFirstLetter = words.groupBy { it.first() }
println(groupedByFirstLetter) // Exibe {c=[cat], d=[dog],
a=[apple, ant]}
```

The method groupBy groups words by their first letter.

Other Operations

Kotlin also supports several other useful operations:

- **find**: Returns the first element that meets a condition.

kotlin

```
val numbers = listOf(1, 2, 3, 4, 5)
val firstEven = numbers.find { it % 2 == 0 }
println(firstEven) // Display 2
```

- **any** and **all**: Check conditions in collection elements.

kotlin

```kotlin
val hasEven = numbers.any { it % 2 == 0 } // Returns true if any
element is even
val allPositive = numbers.all { it > 0 } // Returns true if all are
positive
```

- **reduce** and **fold**: Aggregate values into a single output.

kotlin

```kotlin
val sum = numbers.reduce { acc, num -> acc + num }
println(sum) // Displays 15
```

Sequences and Efficient Processing

When dealing with large data sets, processing each element immediately can be inefficient. Sequences in Kotlin allow for "lazy" processing, evaluating only necessary elements.

Creating Sequences

Sequences can be created from collections or using the generateSequence.

kotlin

```kotlin
val numbers = sequenceOf(1, 2, 3, 4, 5)
```

Sequences can be generated dynamically.

kotlin

```kotlin
val infiniteNumbers = generateSequence(1) { it + 1 }
println(infiniteNumbers.take(5).toList()) // Exibe [1, 2, 3, 4, 5]
```

This code creates an infinite sequence that is limited to the first five numbers.

Lazy Processing (Lazy Evaluation)

Lazy processing optimizes chained operations, performing calculations only when necessary.

kotlin

```
val result = (1..1_000_000).asSequence()
    .filter { it % 2 == 0 }
    .map { it * 2 }
    .take(5)
    .toList()
println(result) // Displays [4, 8, 12, 16, 20]
```

In this example, only the elements necessary to satisfy the method take(5) are processed, reducing resource consumption.

When to Use Sequences

Sequences are useful in scenarios where the collection is very large or when initial processing of the entire collection would be unnecessary. However, for small collections or simple operations, using lists is preferred due to lower management overhead.

Mastery of collections in Kotlin is essential for creating robust and scalable applications. With lists, sets, and maps, you can store and manipulate data efficiently. Operations like filtering, mapping, and grouping make working with collections more intuitive and powerful. For large data scenarios, sequences offer an elegant and optimized solution, ensuring that only the necessary elements are processed. By applying these concepts and techniques, you will be able to manipulate data effectively, promoting code clarity and performance.

CHAPTER 7: CLASSES AND OBJECTS

Kotlin is an object-oriented language that simplifies working with classes and objects. Classes are fundamental blocks that encapsulate data and behavior. Objects are instances of these classes and represent unique entities in the program. The declaration of classes and objects in Kotlin is direct and expressive, allowing you to create flexible and reusable structures.

Declaration of Classes and Objects in Kotlin

Classes are defined with the keyword class, followed by the class name and, optionally, a body that can contain properties and methods.

kotlin

```kotlin
class Person {
    var name: String = ""
    var age : Int = 0

    fun introduce() {
        println("Hi, my name is $name and I am $age years old.")
    }
}
```

The class Person has two properties (name and age) and a method (introduce). To create an object of this class, use the operator ().

kotlin

```kotlin
fun main() {
    val person = Person()
```

```
    person.name = "Alice"
    person.age = 25
    person.introduce()
}
```

The object person is instantiated from the class Person, and the values of its properties are assigned before calling the method introduce.

Classes with Immutable Properties

Properties can be declared as immutable using val. This ensures that its value will not change after initialization.

kotlin

```
class Car(val model: String, val year: Int)
```

Instantiating an object of this class requires providing values for all immutable properties.

kotlin

```
val car = Car("Toyota", 2020)
println("${car.model} - ${car.year}")
```

The code displays the model and year of the car. Since properties are immutable, trying to modify them will result in a compilation error.

Primary and Secondary Builders

Kotlin supports primary and secondary constructors to initialize objects with custom values.

Primary Constructors

The primary constructor is defined directly in the class declaration and can initialize properties.

kotlin

```
class Book(val title: String, val author: String, val pages: Int)
```

The properties title, author and pages are automatically initialized when creating an object.

kotlin

```
val book = Book("Kotlin Essentials", "John Doe", 300)
println("${book.title} by ${book.author}, ${book.pages} pages")
```

This method reduces the need to write redundant code to initialize properties.

Additional Initialization in Constructor

Additional initialization can be performed within the block heat.

kotlin

```
class Circle(val radius: Double) {
    val area: Double

    heat {
        area = Math.PI * radius * radius
    }
}
```

The property area is automatically calculated and initialized after object creation.

kotlin

```
val circle = Circle(5.0)
println("Area: ${circle.area}")
```

Secondary Builders

Secondary constructors are used to provide alternative forms of initialization in addition to the primary constructor. They are declared with the keyword constructor.

kotlin

```kotlin
class Rectangle {
    var width: Int = 0
    var height: Int = 0

    constructor(width: Int, height: Int) {
        this.width = width
        this.height = height
    }
}
```

Width and height values are assigned by the secondary constructor during object creation.

kotlin

```kotlin
val rectangle = Rectangle(10, 5)
println("Width: ${rectangle.width}, Height: $
{rectangle.height}")
```

When using secondary constructors in conjunction with the primary constructor, you can call the primary constructor directly using the keyword this.

kotlin

```kotlin
class Square(size: Int) : Rectangle(size, size)
```

The class Square herd of Rectangle and uses the secondary constructor to initialize a square where width and height are equal.

Properties and Methods

Properties with Getters and Setters

Properties in Kotlin have implicit getters and setters, but can be customized when necessary.

kotlin

```kotlin
class Temperature {
    var celsius: Double = 0.0
        set(value) {
            field = if (value >= -273.15) value else -273.15
        }
        get() = field
}
```

The property celsius has a custom setter that prevents values below absolute zero.

kotlin

```kotlin
val temp = Temperature()
temp.celsius = -300.0
println(temp.celsius) // Displays -273.15
```

The getter returns the stored value, while the setter applies a check before assigning the value.

Methods

Methods in Kotlin can manipulate or access class properties.

kotlin

```kotlin
class BankAccount(var balance: Double) {
    fun deposit(amount: Double) {
        if (amount > 0) balance += amount
    }

    fun withdraw(amount: Double) {
        if (amount > 0 && amount <= balance) balance -= amount
    }
}
```

This class has methods for depositing and withdrawing money, ensuring that operations are valid.

kotlin

```kotlin
val account = BankAccount(100.0)
account.deposit(50.0)
account.withdraw(30.0)
println("Balance: ${account.balance}")
```

The methods manipulate the balance according to defined rules.

Static Methods

Methods that do not depend on an instance can be defined within a block companion object.

kotlin

```kotlin
class MathUtils {
    companion object {
        fun square(number: Int) = number * number
    }
}
```

The method square can be called directly by the class name.

kotlin

```kotlin
println(MathUtils.square(5)) // Displays 25
```

Method Overloading

Kotlin allows you to define multiple methods with the same name, as long as their signatures are different.

kotlin

```kotlin
class Printer {
    fun print(value: String) {
```

```
    println("String: $value")
  }

  fun print(value: Int) {
    println("Int: $value")
  }
}
```

The correct method will be chosen based on the type of the argument.

kotlin

```
val printer = Printer()
printer.print("Hello")
printer.print(123)
```

Data Classes

Kotlin has functionality called data classes, which are ideal for representing data models.

kotlin

```
data class User(val name: String, val age: Int)
```

These classes automatically provide methods like toString, equals, hashCode and copy.

kotlin

```
val user = User("Alice", 25)
println(user) // Exibe User(name=Alice, age=25)
```

The method copy creates a new instance with the same properties, but allows you to modify them.

kotlin

```
val updatedUser = user.copy(age = 26)
```

```
println(updatedUser) // Exibe User(name=Alice, age=26)
```

Kotlin makes working with classes and objects easier by offering modern, idiomatic tools for encapsulating data and behavior. The combination of primary and secondary constructors, properties with custom getters and setters, and static or instance methods promotes flexibility and clarity. Data classes simplify working with models, while features like overloading and extension methods increase the expressiveness of the code. These fundamentals make Kotlin a powerful language for object-oriented development.

CHAPTER 8: INHERITANCE AND POLYMORPHISM

Inheritance and polymorphism are fundamental concepts in object-oriented programming, and Kotlin provides robust tools to implement them simply and efficiently. Inheritance allows one class to reuse the properties and methods of another, while polymorphism allows different classes to share a common interface, promoting flexibility and code reuse.

The Modifier open for Heritage

By default, classes in Kotlin are final, that is, they cannot be inherited. To allow a class to be extended, the modifier open must be used.

kotlin

```kotlin
open class Animal {
    open fun speak() {
        println("Animal makes a sound")
    }
}
```

The class Animal is marked as open, allowing other classes to inherit it. The method speak is also open, indicating that it can be overridden in subclasses.

Derived Classes

A derived class is created using the colon : followed by the name of the base class.

kotlin

```kotlin
class Dog : Animal() {
    override fun speak() {
        println("Dog barks")
    }
}
```

The class Dog herd of Animal and override the method speak to provide your own implementation.

kotlin

```kotlin
fun main() {
    val animal = Animal()
    animal.speak() // Exibe "Animal makes a sound"

    val dog = Dog()
    dog.speak() // Exibe "Dog barks"
}
```

The method call speak in an object of type Dog executes the overridden version in the derived class.

Overridden Methods

Methods in a base class can be overridden in a derived class to modify or extend its behavior. The modifier override is mandatory and ensures that the overridden method corresponds to a method defined in the base class.

kotlin

```kotlin
open class Shape {
    open fun area(): Double {
        return 0.0
    }
}

class Circle(val radius: Double) : Shape() {
    override fun area(): Double {
```

```
        return Math.PI * radius * radius
    }
}
```

The class Circle herd of Shape and provides its own implementation for calculating area.

kotlin

```
val circle = Circle(5.0)
println("Area of the circle: ${circle.area()}") // Exibe "Area of the circle: 78.53981633974483"
```

The specific implementation of area in the derived class is used instead of the default implementation.

Overridden Properties

Properties can also be overridden in derived classes, following the same method pattern.

kotlin

```
open class Vehicle {
    open val speed: Int = 60
}

class SportsCar : Vehicle() {
    override val speed: Int = 200
}
```

The value of the property speed is different in the derived class.

kotlin

```
val car = SportsCar()
println("Speed: ${car.speed} km/h") // Exibe "Speed: 200 km/h"
```

Practical Applications of Polymorphism

Polymorphism allows objects from different derived classes to be treated as instances of their base class. This is useful for creating flexible systems that process different types of objects uniformly.

Example of Polymorphism

kotlin

```kotlin
open class Employee(val name: String) {
    open fun calculateSalary(): Double {
        return 3000.0
    }
}

class Manager(name: String, val bonus: Double) :
Employee(name) {
    override fun calculateSalary(): Double {
        return super.calculateSalary() + bonus
    }
}

class Developer(name: String, val overtimeHours: Int) :
Employee(name) {
    override fun calculateSalary(): Double {
        return super.calculateSalary() + (overtimeHours * 50)
    }
}
```

As classes Manager and Developer extend Employee and provide different salary calculation implementations.

kotlin

```kotlin
fun printSalaries(employees: List<Employee>) {
    for (employee in employees) {
        println("${employee.name}: $
{employee.calculateSalary()}")
    }
```

```
}
val employees = listOf(
    Manager("Alice", 2000.0),
    Developer("Bob", 10),
    Employee("Charlie")
)
printSalaries(employees)
```

The method printSalaries accepts a list of objects of type Employee, but calls the correct implementation of calculateSalary based on the actual type of the object.

Using Abstract Classes

Abstract classes are used as templates for derived classes and cannot be instantiated directly. Abstract methods and properties have no implementation and must be overridden.

kotlin

```
abstract class Appliance {
    abstract fun turnOn()
    abstract fun turnOff()
}

class WashingMachine : Appliance() {
    override fun turnOn() {
        println("Washing machine is now ON")
    }

    override fun turnOff() {
        println("Washing machine is now OFF")
    }
}
```

The class Appliance defines the contract for its subclasses.

kotlin

```kotlin
val machine = WashingMachine()
machine.turnOn() // Exibe "Washing machine is now ON"
machine.turnOff() // Exibe "Washing machine is now OFF"
```

Interfaces and Polymorphism

Interfaces are similar to abstract classes, but allow the implementation of multiple interfaces in a single class.

kotlin

```kotlin
interface Flyable {
    fun fly()
}

interface Swimable {
    fun swim()
}

class Duck : Flyable, Swimable {
    override fun fly() {
        println("Duck is flying")
    }

    override fun swim() {
        println("Duck is swimming")
    }
}
```

The class Duck implements both Flyable How much Swimable.

kotlin

```kotlin
val duck = Duck()
duck.fly() // Exibe "Duck is flying"
duck.swim() // Exibe "Duck is swimming"
```

Interfaces promote reuse and composition of behaviors, allowing different classes to share the same functionality.

Combination of Inheritance and Polymorphism

Inheritance and polymorphism together promote code reuse and flexibility, allowing systems to be extended without significant changes. In real systems, such as games or enterprise applications, these tools are often used to implement object hierarchies or dynamic processes.

Example: Payment System
kotlin

```kotlin
abstract class PaymentProcessor {
    abstract fun processPayment(amount: Double)
}

class CreditCardProcessor : PaymentProcessor() {
    override fun processPayment(amount: Double) {
        println("Processing credit card payment of $$amount")
    }
}

class PayPalProcessor : PaymentProcessor() {
    override fun processPayment(amount: Double) {
        println("Processing PayPal payment of $$amount")
    }
}
```

The system accepts different payment methods, treated in a uniform manner.

kotlin

```kotlin
fun processAllPayments(processors: List<PaymentProcessor>,
amount: Double) {
    for (processor in processors) {
        processor.processPayment(amount)
    }
}
```

```
val processors = listOf(CreditCardProcessor(),
PayPalProcessor())
processAllPayments(processors, 100.0)
```

The code processes payments using different processors without modifying the main flow.

Inheritance and polymorphism are essential for creating extensible, reusable, and organized systems. With the use of the modifier open, overridden methods and derived classes, it is possible to implement effective and adaptable solutions. Polymorphism promotes flexibility by allowing different objects to share a common interface while maintaining their unique behavior. These concepts become even more powerful when combined with abstract classes and interfaces, ensuring that code remains modular and prepared for changes.

CHAPTER 9: INTERFACES AND ABSTRACT CLASSES

Interfaces and abstract classes are fundamental tools in Kotlin to promote abstraction, modularity, and code reuse. Understanding the differences between these two concepts is essential to creating robust and flexible systems. This chapter explores the characteristics of each, shows how to use them effectively, and provides guidelines for best practices in developing with abstractions.

Differences Between Interfaces and Abstract Classes

Although both structures are used to define behaviors that other classes can implement, they have fundamental differences.

Abstract Classes

1. **Definition and Usage**
   Abstract classes are designed to serve as templates for other classes. They can contain methods and properties with or without implementation.
2. **Heritage**
   Abstract classes can only be inherited by a single class, due to the single inheritance restriction.
3. **State**
   They can contain stateful properties, such as variables that hold internal values.
4. **Visibility Modifier**
   Allow the use of visibility modifiers, such as protected, which restrict access to derived classes.

kotlin

```kotlin
abstract class Vehicle(val name: String) {
    abstract fun move()

    fun description() {
        println("$name is a vehicle.")
    }
}
```

The class Vehicle defines an abstract method move and a concrete method description.

Interfaces

1. **Definition and Usage**
   Interfaces are used to define contracts that classes must follow. All methods declared in an interface are, by default, abstract, unless they contain a default implementation.

2. **Multiple Inheritance**
   A class can implement multiple interfaces, overcoming the limitation of single inheritance.

3. **Stateless**
   Interfaces cannot store state directly. Properties in interfaces must be abstract or have calculated values.

4. **Optional Implementation**
   Methods in interfaces can have a default implementation, but it is not mandatory.

kotlin

```kotlin
interface Flyable {
    fun fly()

    fun checkWings() {
        println("Wings are in good condition.")
    }
}
```

A interface Flyable defines an abstract method fly and a method with standard implementation checkWings.

General Comparison

Feature	Abstract Class	Interface
Inheritance Support	Unique heritage	Multiple inheritance
State	Allows stateful properties	Does not allow direct status
Concrete Methods	Permitted	Permitted
Use of protected	Yes	No

Creating Reusable Contracts with Interfaces

Interfaces are ideal for creating reusable contracts that define the expected behavior of classes, regardless of their hierarchy.

Simple Implementation

kotlin

```kotlin
interface Drivable {
    fun drive()
}
```

A class that implements this interface must provide an implementation for the method drive.

kotlin

```kotlin
class Car : Drivable {
    override fun drive() {
        println("The car is driving.")
    }
}
```

The class Car now follows the contract defined by Drivable.

kotlin

```
val car = Car()
car.drive() // Exibe "The car is driving."
```

Multiple Interfaces

Kotlin allows a class to implement multiple interfaces, increasing its flexibility.

kotlin

```
interface Floatable {
    fun float()
}

class AmphibiousCar : Drivable, Floatable {
    override fun drive() {
        println("The amphibious car is driving.")
    }

    override fun float() {
        println("The amphibious car is floating.")
    }
}
```

The class AmphibiousCar implements both Drivable How much Floatable, displaying behaviors for both contracts.

kotlin

```
val amphibiousCar = AmphibiousCar()
amphibiousCar.drive() // Exibe "The amphibious car is driving."
amphibiousCar.float() // Exibe "The amphibious car is floating."
```

Interfaces with Properties

Properties in interfaces are declared as abstract or with calculated values.

kotlin

```
interface Identifiable {
    val id: String
}
```

```
class Product(override val id: String) : Identifiable
```

The property id **must be provided by the class that implements the interface.**

kotlin

```
val product = Product("12345")
println("Product ID: ${product.id}") // Exibe "Product ID: 12345"
```

Using Standard Methods

Interfaces can include methods with standard implementations, reducing the effort required to implement derived classes.

kotlin

```
interface Printable {
    fun print() {
        println("Printing...")
    }
}
```

```
class Document : Printable
```

The class Document **inherits the default implementation of the method** print.

kotlin

```
val document = Document()
document.print() // Exibe "Printing..."
```

Good Practices in Using Abstractions in Kotlin

1. **Choose Between Interface and Abstract Class**
   Use interfaces to define broadly reusable contracts and abstract classes when you need to share common state or behavior between classes.
2. **Avoid Inheritance Overhead**
   If a class needs to inherit multiple concrete implementations, consider splitting the responsibilities into smaller interfaces.
3. **Prefer Standard Methods Whenever Possible**
   Methods with standard implementations in interfaces allow the extension of functionality without breaking existing contracts.
4. **Apply the Interface Segregation Principle**
   Break down large interfaces into smaller, more specific ones.

kotlin

```kotlin
interface Scanner {
    fun scan()
}

interface Printer {
    fun print()
}

class MultiFunctionDevice : Scanner, Printer {
    override fun scan() {
        println("Scanning document...")
    }

    override fun print() {
        println("Printing document...")
    }
}
```

Separating into smaller interfaces makes the design more modular.

5. **Use Sealed Classes for Tight Control**
   Sealed classes can be used in conjunction with abstractions to limit hierarchies to a fixed set of types.

kotlin

```kotlin
sealed class Operation {
    abstract fun execute(): Int
}

class Addition(val a: Int, val b: Int) : Operation() {
    override fun execute() = a + b
}

class Subtraction(val a: Int, val b: Int) : Operation() {
    override fun execute() = a - b
}
```

The class Operation is sealed, ensuring that only its subclasses can be used.

kotlin

```kotlin
val operation: Operation = Addition(5, 3)
println(operation.execute()) // Displays 8
```

6. **Document Your Abstractions**
   Interfaces and abstract classes often define broad behaviors. Add clear comments to explain your purpose.

Interfaces and abstract classes are powerful tools for creating flexible, well-organized systems. By understanding their differences and using them appropriately, you can create more modular, reusable, and scalable code. Good practices in abstraction design ensure that your system is easy to maintain and extend in the future.

CHAPTER 10: WORKING WITH STRINGS

Strings are an essential part of any programming language, used to store and manipulate text. Kotlin offers several tools for working with strings efficiently, from basic operations like concatenation and manipulation to advanced features like multiline strings, interpolation, and built-in methods that simplify textual processing.

Basic and Advanced String Manipulation

Strings in Kotlin are immutable, which means any modification creates a new string instance. This provides safety and avoids unwanted side effects.

String Declaration

Strings are declared using double quotes.

kotlin

```
val greeting = "Hello, Kotlin!"
```

Concatenation

Strings can be concatenated using the operator +.

kotlin

```
val firstName = "John"
val lastName = "Doe"
val fullName = firstName + " " + lastName
println(fullName) // Displays "John Doe"
```

Concatenation is useful for combining textual values, but it can be replaced by interpolation, which is more efficient and readable.

Accessing Characters

Characters in a string can be accessed by indices, starting at 0.

kotlin

```
val text = "Kotlin"
println(text[0]) // Displays "K"
println(text[5]) // Displays "n"
```

Substrings

The method substring is used to extract parts of a string.

kotlin

```
val phrase = "Hello, Kotlin!"
val subPhrase = phrase.substring(7, 13)
println(subPhrase) // Displays "Kotlin"
```

The starting index is inclusive while the ending index is exclusive.

String Size

The size of a string is obtained through the property length.

kotlin

```
val word = "Programming"
println("Length: ${word.length}") // Exibe "Length: 11"
```

String Comparison

Strings can be compared using the operators == or equals.

kotlin

```
val a = "kotlin"
val b = "Kotlin"
```

```kotlin
println(a == b) // Displays "false"
println(a.equals(b, ignoreCase = true)) // Exibe "true"
```

The option ignoreCase allows you to compare strings ignoring case differences.

Using Multiline and Interpolated Strings

Strings Multilinhas

Multiline strings are declared using three double quotes """.

kotlin

```kotlin
val multiLineString = """
    Kotlin is a modern language.
    It is concise, expressive, and safe.
"""
println(multiLineString)
```

This type of string preserves line breaks and additional spaces, but can be formatted using the method trimMargin.

kotlin

```kotlin
val formattedString = """
    |Kotlin is a modern language.
    |It is concise, expressive, and safe.
""".trimMargin()
println(formattedString)
```

The method trimMargin removes margins prefixed by a specific character, such as |.

String Interpolation

Interpolation allows you to insert values or expressions directly into a string, using the symbol $.

kotlin

```
val name = "Alice"
val age = 30
val message = "Name: $name, Age: $age"
println(message) // Exibe "Name: Alice, Age: 30"
```

More complex expressions can be entered using ${}.

kotlin

```
choose x = 10
value y = 20
println("Sum of $x and $y is ${x + y}") // Exibe "Sum of 10 and
20 is 30"
```

Interpolation improves readability and reduces the need to manually concatenate strings.

Useful Methods for String Processing

Kotlin offers several inbuilt methods to manipulate strings efficiently.

Changing Case Letters

The methods toUpperCase and toLowerCase convert strings to uppercase or lowercase.

kotlin

```
val text = "Hello"
println(text.toUpperCase()) // Displays "HELLO"
println(text.toLowerCase()) // Exibe "hello"
```

String Division

The method split splits a string into parts based on a delimiter.

kotlin

```
val csv = "Kotlin,Java,Python"
val languages = csv.split(",")
```

```kotlin
println(languages) // Display [Kotlin, Java, Python]
```

The result is a list of strings.

Text Replacement

The method replace replaces parts of a string.

kotlin

```kotlin
val sentence = "Kotlin is awesome!"
val modifiedSentence = sentence.replace("awesome",
"powerful")
println(modifiedSentence) // Exibe "Kotlin is powerful!"
```

The method can also be used with regular expressions.

Containment Checks

The methods contains, startsWith and endsWith check for the presence of substrings or patterns.

kotlin

```kotlin
val text = "Kotlin programming"
println(text.contains("program")) // Displays "true"
println(text.startsWith("Kot")) // Exibe "true"
println(text.endsWith("ing")) // Displays "true"
```

Space Removal

The methods trim, trimStart and trimEnd remove whitespace from the beginning, end, or entire string.

kotlin

```kotlin
val rawText = "  Kotlin  "
println(rawText.trim()) // Displays "Kotlin"
```

String Reversal

The method reversed reverses the order of characters.

kotlin

```
val text = "Kotlin"
println(text.reversed()) // Displays "niltoK"
```

String Grouping

The method chunked splits the string into smaller parts of fixed size.

kotlin

```
val data="abcdefghij"
val chunks = data.chunked(3)
println(chunks) // Exibe [abc, def, ghi, j]
```

Processing with Regular Expressions

Strings can be processed with regular expressions for advanced search and replacement.

kotlin

```
val input = "abc123def456"
val numbers = "\\d+".toRegex().findAll(input).map { it.value }
println(numbers.toList()) // Exibe [123, 456]
```

The method toRegex converts a string to a regular expression.

Iteration over Characters

Strings can be traversed character by character using a loop for.

kotlin

```
val text = "Kotlin"
for (char in text) {
    println(char)
}
```

Each character in the string is displayed individually.

Advanced Formatting

Formatted strings can be created with the method String.format.

kotlin

```
val pi = 3.14159
println("Value of Pi: %.2f".format(pi)) // Exibe "Value of Pi:
3.14"
```

Additional formats, such as %d for integers and %s for strings, they allow you to customize the output.

Good Practices When Working with Strings

1. **Use Interpolation Whenever Possible**
   Interpolation is more readable and less error-prone than manual concatenation.
2. **Avoid Creating Strings in Loops**
   Creating multiple instances of strings in a loop can be inefficient. Use StringBuilder or StringBuffer for extensive manipulations.

kotlin

```
val builder = StringBuilder()
for (i in 1..5) {
    builder.append("Number: $i\n")
}
println(builder.toString())
```

3. **Use Embedded Methods**
   Take advantage of Kotlin's string methods to avoid writing unnecessary logic.
4. **Consider Immutability**
   Strings are immutable, which makes them safe to share between threads. Use this to your advantage to

avoid unwanted side effects.

Strings in Kotlin are powerful and flexible, offering a comprehensive set of tools for basic and advanced manipulation. With support for interpolation, multiline strings, and powerful built-in methods, you can create clean and robust solutions for text processing. Applying good practices guarantees more readable, efficient and easier to maintain code.

CHAPTER 11: FILE OPERATIONS

File management is an essential skill in many applications. In Kotlin, it is possible to perform file reading and writing operations in a simple and efficient way, using the standard library or other complementary APIs. This chapter covers how to work with text and binary files, manipulate streams and buffers, and implement best practices for dealing with large files.

Reading and Writing Files in Kotlin

The Kotlin standard library provides direct methods for reading and writing files, taking advantage of the Java API features.

Reading Text Files

The method readText is used to read the entire contents of a file as a single string.

kotlin

```kotlin
import java.io.File

fun readFile(fileName: String): String {
    val file = File(fileName)
    return file.readText()
}

fun main() {
    val content = readFile("example.txt")
    println(content)
}
```

This code reads the entire contents of the file example.txt and displays it in the console.

Line by Line Reading

To process large files without loading the entire content into memory, the method readLines reads the file line by line and returns a list of strings.

kotlin

```kotlin
fun readLines(fileName: String): List<String> {
    val file = File(fileName)
    return file.readLines()
}

fun main() {
    val lines = readLines("example.txt")
    lines.forEach { println(it) }
}
```

The method forEach loops through each line of the list and prints it. This is useful for analyzing or processing data in large files.

Writing in Files

The method writeText writes a string to a file, overwriting the existing content.

kotlin

```kotlin
fun writeFile(fileName: String, content: String) {
    val file = File(fileName)
    file.writeText(content)
}

fun main() {
    writeFile("output.txt", "This is an example of writing to a file.")
    println("File written successfully.")
}
```

The code creates a file output.txt and inserts the specified text.

Adding Content to a File

To add content to the end of a file without overwriting the existing one, use the method appendText.

kotlin

```
fun appendToFile(fileName: String, content: String) {
    val file = File(fileName)
    file.appendText(content)
}

fun main() {
    appendToFile("output.txt", "\nAdditional line added.")
    println("Content appended successfully.")
}
```

This method is useful when you need to record logs or add incremental information to a file.

Manipulating Binary Files

Binary files can be read and written using readBytes and writeBytes.

kotlin

```
fun copyBinaryFile(source: String, destination: String) {
    val inputFile = File(source)
    val outputFile = File(destination)
    val bytes = inputFile.readBytes()
    outputFile.writeBytes(bytes)
}

fun main() {
    copyBinaryFile("image.jpg", "image_copy.jpg")
    println("Binary file copied successfully.")
}
```

The method readBytes reads the file as a byte array, which can be manipulated or copied to another file.

Working with Streams and Buffers

Streams and buffers offer an efficient way to process data, especially in large files. They allow data to be read or written in smaller blocks, reducing memory usage.

Reading with BufferedReader

THE BufferedReader reads data in blocks, which is more efficient than loading the entire file into memory at once.

kotlin

```kotlin
import java.io.BufferedReader
import java.io.FileReader

fun readFileWithBufferedReader(fileName: String) {
    BufferedReader(FileReader(fileName)).use { reader ->
        var line = reader.readLine()
        while (line != null) {
            println(line)
            line = reader.readLine()
        }
    }
}

fun main() {
    readFileWithBufferedReader("example.txt")
}
```

The method use guarantees that the resource will be closed automatically after use, preventing memory leaks.

Writing with BufferedWriter

THE BufferedWriter writes data in blocks,

optimizing the writing process for large files.

kotlin

```kotlin
import java.io.BufferedWriter
import java.io.FileWriter

fun writeFileWithBufferedWriter(fileName: String, content:
List<String>) {
    BufferedWriter(FileWriter(fileName)).use { writer ->
        content.forEach { line ->
            writer.write(line)
            writer.newLine() // Adds a new line after each content
        }
    }
}

fun main() {
    val content = listOf("Line 1", "Line 2", "Line 3")
    writeFileWithBufferedWriter("buffered_output.txt",
content)
    println("File written with BufferedWriter successfully.")
}
```

This code uses the BufferedWriter to write multiple lines to a file. The method newLine adds a line break after each content.

Streams for Binary Manipulation

To read and write binary files in blocks, we use InputStream and OutputStream.

kotlin

```kotlin
import java.io.FileInputStream
import java.io.FileOutputStream

fun copyBinaryWithStreams(source: String, destination:
String) {
    FileInputStream(source).use { input ->
```

```
FileOutputStream(destination).use { output ->
   val buffer = ByteArray(1024)
   var bytesRead = input.read(buffer)
   while (bytesRead != -1) {
      output.write(buffer, 0, bytesRead)
      bytesRead = input.read(buffer)
   }
  }
 }
}

fun main() {
   copyBinaryWithStreams("large_file.dat",
"large_file_copy.dat")
   println("Binary file copied with streams successfully.")
}
```

In this example, the file is processed in blocks of 1024 bytes, optimizing memory used and execution time.

Best Practices for Handling Large Files

1. **Use Streams to Avoid Memory Issues**
   When handling large files, use streams or buffers to process data in chunks rather than loading the whole thing into memory.
2. **Close Resources with use**
   Use the method use to automatically manage the closure of streams or readers. This prevents memory leaks and errors related to open files.
3. **Break Complex Operations into Smaller Functions**
   Break extensive operations into smaller, simpler functions like reading, processing, and writing.

kotlin

```
fun processFile(inputFile: String, outputFile: String, process:
(String) -> String) {
```

```kotlin
File(inputFile).bufferedReader().use { reader ->
    File(outputFile).bufferedWriter().use { writer ->
        reader.forEachLine { line ->
            writer.write(process(line))
            writer.newLine()
        }
    }
}
```

This code applies a transformation to each line of an input file and writes the result to an output file.

4. **Handle Exceptions When Working with Files**
   Always handle exceptions to handle errors such as missing files or insufficient permissions.

kotlin

```kotlin
fun safeFileOperation(fileName: String) {
    try {
        val content = File(fileName).readText()
        println(content)
    } catch (e: Exception) {
        println("Error reading file: ${e.message}")
    }
}
```

5. **Prefer Modern APIs Whenever Possible**
   Kotlin standard library functions are more idiomatic and often safer than Java methods.
6. **Avoid Overwriting Files Without Warning**
   Verify that the target file exists before overwriting its contents.

kotlin

```kotlin
fun safeWriteFile(fileName: String, content: String) {
```

```kotlin
    val file = File(fileName)
    if (file.exists()) {
        println("File already exists. Skipping write operation.")
        return
    }
    file.writeText(content)
}
```

7. **Use Compression When Necessary**
   When dealing with large volumes of data, consider compressing files to save disk space and improve transfer speed.

kotlin

```kotlin
import java.util.zip.GZIPOutputStream

fun compressFile(source: String, destination: String) {
    FileInputStream(source).use { input ->
        GZIPOutputStream(FileOutputStream(destination)).use
{ output ->
            input.copyTo(output)
        }
    }
}

fun main() {
    compressFile("large_file.txt", "large_file.gz")
    println("File compressed successfully.")
}
```

Compression reduces file size and is useful for backups or transmission over a network.

8. **Avoid Unnecessary Processing**
   Filter or process only relevant data when working with large files, rather than analyzing the entire file.

kotlin

```kotlin
fun countLinesWithKeyword(fileName: String, keyword:
String): Int {
    return File(fileName).useLines { lines ->
        lines.count { it.contains(keyword) }
    }
}
```

This code only counts lines that contain a specific keyword, ignoring the others.

Working with files in Kotlin is intuitive and efficient, thanks to integration with modern APIs and the simplicity of the standard library. From basic operations, such as reading and writing text, to advanced manipulations with streams and buffers, Kotlin provides tools that meet diverse needs. Applying good practices ensures that the code is safe, efficient and prepared to deal with large volumes of data.

CHAPTER 12: EXCEPTION HANDLING

Exception handling is essential to ensure that applications handle errors in a controlled and predictable manner. Kotlin, as a modern language, offers robust tools for identifying and handling errors, including blocks try, catch and finally. Additionally, it allows you to create custom exceptions and use best practices to minimize common code failures.

Identification and Treatment of Errors
with try, catch and finally

The Block try-catch

The block try-catch is used to catch and handle exceptions that may occur during code execution.

kotlin

```kotlin
fun divide(a: Int, b: Int): Int {
    return try {
        a / b
    } catch (e: ArithmeticException) {
        println("Error: Division by zero is not allowed.")
        0
    }
}
```

In the example, the code tries to perform the division. Case b is equal to zero, one ArithmeticException is launched and captured in the block catch.

kotlin

```kotlin
fun main() {
```

```
val result = divide(10, 0)
println("Result: $result")
}
```

The output displays the error message and a default value to avoid interrupting the program.

The Block finally

The block finally is executed every time, regardless of whether an exception was thrown or not. It is useful for freeing up resources or taking final actions.

kotlin

```
fun readFile(fileName: String) {
    val file = java.io.File(fileName)
    try {
        println(file.readText())
    } catch (e: Exception) {
        println("Error: ${e.message}")
    } finally {
        println("Closing file resources.")
    }
}
```

Even if an exception occurs while reading the file, the block finally ensures that resources are released.

kotlin

```
readFile("nonexistent.txt")
```

The error message is displayed, followed by the execution of the block finally.

Catching Multiple Exceptions

Blocks catch can be stacked to handle different types of exceptions.

kotlin

```kotlin
fun handleMultipleExceptions(input: String) {
    try {
        val number = input.toInt()
        println("Number: $number")
    } catch (e: NumberFormatException) {
        println("Error: Input is not a valid number.")
    } catch (e: Exception) {
        println("Unexpected error: ${e.message}")
    }
}
```

The code tries to convert a string to a number. If the string is not valid, the appropriate exception will be handled.

kotlin

```kotlin
handleMultipleExceptions("abc")
```

The first block catch catches the specific invalid format exception, while the second handles any other unexpected errors.

Custom Exceptions

Kotlin allows you to create custom exceptions to handle specific scenarios. This promotes clarity and consistency in the code.

Creating an Exception Class

A custom exception class inherits from Exception or one of its subclasses.

kotlin

```kotlin
class InvalidInputException(message: String) :
Exception(message)
```

This class represents an exception for invalid input. The builder receives a descriptive message.

Throwing Custom Exceptions

The operator throw is used to throw custom exceptions.

kotlin

```kotlin
fun validateInput(input: Int) {
    if (input < 0) {
        throw InvalidInputException("Input must be non-negative.")
    }
    println("Valid input: $input")
}
```

The method validateInput throws a custom exception if the given value is negative.

kotlin

```kotlin
try {
    validateInput(-5)
} catch (e: InvalidInputException) {
    println("Error: ${e.message}")
}
```

The block catch catches the exception and displays the corresponding message.

Using Custom Exceptions in Complex Flows

Custom exceptions are useful in more advanced scenarios, such as validations across layers or services.

kotlin

```kotlin
class UserNotFoundException(message: String) :
Exception(message)

fun findUser(userId: Int): String {
```

```
    if (userId != 1) {
        throw UserNotFoundException("User with ID $userId not
found.")
    }
    return "User found: John Doe"
}
```

When calling the method findUser, an exception is thrown if the user is not found.

kotlin

```
try {
    println(findUser(2))
} catch (e: UserNotFoundException) {
    println("Error: ${e.message}")
}
```

This approach provides more meaningful and specific error messages.

Strategies to Avoid Common Mistakes

Validate Data Before Processing

Validating inputs early in processing reduces the likelihood of unexpected exceptions.

kotlin

```
fun divideSafely(a: Int, b: Int): Int {
    require(b != 0) { "Denominator must not be zero." }
    return a / b
}
```

The method require launch a IllegalArgumentException if the condition is not met.

kotlin

```
try {
    println(divideSafely(10, 0))
} catch (e: IllegalArgumentException) {
    println("Error: ${e.message}")
}
```

Use try As Expression

The block try can return values, simplifying error handling.

kotlin

```
fun parseNumber(input: String): Int {
    return try {
        input.toInt()
    } catch (e: NumberFormatException) {
        0
    }
}
```

If the conversion fails, the method returns a default value instead of throwing an exception.

kotlin

```
println(parseNumber("abc")) // Displays 0
```

Avoid Catching Generic Exceptions

Handle specific exceptions whenever possible rather than catching Exception or Throwable indiscriminately. This promotes clarity and reduces the risk of hiding errors.

kotlin

```
try {
    val data = listOf(1, 2, 3)
    println(data[5])
} catch (e: IndexOutOfBoundsException) {
```

```
    println("Error: Index out of bounds.")
}
```

This approach directly addresses the problem without masking other potential exceptions.

Use Resources with use

When manipulating resources such as files or streams, use the use to ensure automatic closing.

kotlin

```
fun readFileSafely(fileName: String): String {
    return File(fileName).bufferedReader().use { it.readText() }
}
```

This practice prevents resource leaks, even in the case of exceptions.

Record Logs for Debugging

Recording detailed logs is essential for identifying and correcting errors. Use libraries like Log4j or slf4j to integrate professional logs into your project.

kotlin

```
fun processTransaction(amount: Int) {
    try {
        require(amount > 0) { "Transaction amount must be
positive." }
        println("Processing transaction of $amount units.")
    } catch (e: IllegalArgumentException) {
        println("Error: ${e.message}")
        // log.error("Transaction failed: ${e.message}")
    }
}
```

Adding clear messages in the log helps with debugging and

further analysis.

Prefer Exceptions Over Silent Returns

When something goes wrong, throwing an exception is more informative than returning values silently.

kotlin

```kotlin
fun authenticate(user: String?, password: String?): Boolean {
    requireNotNull(user) { "User must not be null." }
    requireNotNull(password) { "Password must not be null." }

    if (user == "admin" && password == "1234") {
        return true
    } else {
        throw SecurityException("Invalid credentials.")
    }
}
```

This approach reduces ambiguities and makes the code more resilient.

Avoid Propagation of Unhandled Exceptions

Wrap critical methods with handling blocks to prevent exceptions from propagating uncontrollably.

kotlin

```kotlin
fun executeTask() {
    try {
        performTask()
    } catch (e: Exception) {
        println("Task execution failed: ${e.message}")
    }
}

fun performTask() {
    throw RuntimeException("Unexpected error during task execution.")
```

}

This practice maintains system stability even when errors occur.

Handling exceptions correctly is a fundamental skill in any robust application. Using try, catch and finally effectively, combined with good practices, it is possible to create reliable systems, capable of dealing with errors in a predictable way. Custom exceptions and strategies such as early validation, use of logs, and efficient resource management ensure that code is more secure, readable, and easier to maintain.

CHAPTER 13: OBJECT-ORIENTED PROGRAMMING

Object Oriented Programming (OOP) is one of the most widely used paradigms in software development. Kotlin, as a modern and robust language, fully supports fundamental OOP concepts such as encapsulation, inheritance, and polymorphism. Additionally, its simplified syntax makes implementing popular design patterns more accessible and efficient.

Review of OOP Fundamental Concepts

Classes and Objects

In POO, a **class** is a model that defines the characteristics and behaviors of an object. One **object** is an instance of this class.

kotlin

```kotlin
class Person(val name: String, var age: Int) {
    fun introduce() {
        println("Hi, I'm $name and I'm $age years old.")
    }
}

fun main() {
    val person = Person("Alice", 30)
    person.introduce()  // Exibe "Hi, I'm Alice and I'm 30 years old."
}
```

The class Person defines two properties (name and age) and a method (introduce) that allows the object to present itself.

Encapsulation

THE **encapsulation** is the principle of restricting direct access to the internal components of a class, exposing only what is necessary. In Kotlin, this is done with visibility modifiers like private, protected, internal and public.

kotlin

```kotlin
class BankAccount(private var balance: Double) {
    fun deposit(amount: Double) {
        if (amount > 0) balance += amount
    }

    fun getBalance(): Double {
        return balance
    }
}
```

The property balance is private and can only be manipulated through the methods deposit and getBalance.

kotlin

```kotlin
val account = BankAccount(100.0)
account.deposit(50.0)
println(account.getBalance()) // Displays 150.0
```

Heritage

A **heritage** allows one class to reuse the properties and methods of another. In Kotlin, this is accomplished with the modifier open in the base class and the operator : to the derived class.

kotlin

```kotlin
open class Animal(val name: String) {
    open fun speak() {
        println("$name makes a sound.")
    }
```

```
}

class Dog(name: String) : Animal(name) {
    override fun speak() {
        println("$name barks.")
    }
}
```

The class Dog herd of Animal and override the method speak.

kotlin

```
val dog = Dog("Buddy")
dog.speak() // Exibe "Buddy barks."
```

Polymorphism

THE **polymorphism** allows methods and properties of derived classes to be accessed uniformly through base class references.

kotlin

```
val animals: List<Animal> = listOf(Animal("Generic"),
Dog("Buddy"))
animals.forEach { it.speak() }
```

Even though animals be a list of Animal, the method speak calls the specific implementation of the class Dog for objects of this class.

Applying Encapsulation, Inheritance and Polymorphism in Kotlin

Encapsulation with Custom Getters and Setters

Getters and setters can be customized to add logic when accessing or modifying properties.

kotlin

```
class Rectangle(var width: Int, var height: Int) {
```

```
    var area: Int
      get() = width * height
      set(value) {
          width = value / height
      }
}
```

The getter calculates the area automatically, while the setter adjusts the width based on the height.

kotlin

```
val rectangle = Rectangle(10, 5)
println(rectangle.area) // Displays 50
rectangle.area = 100
println(rectangle.width) // Exibe 20
```

Inheritance with Advanced Initialization

Kotlin supports advanced initialization in classes derived through the primary constructor.

kotlin

```
open class Employee(val name: String, val id: Int)

class Manager(name: String, id: Int, val department: String) :
Employee(name, id)
```

The class Manager initializes the base class properties and adds a specific property.

kotlin

```
val manager = Manager("Alice", 101, "HR")
println("${manager.name} manages ${manager.department}.")
```

Polymorphism and Abstract Classes

Abstract classes can be used to define generic contracts, allowing derived classes to implement specific behavior.

kotlin

```kotlin
abstract class Shape {
    abstract fun calculateArea(): Double
}

class Circle(val radius: Double) : Shape() {
    override fun calculateArea(): Double = Math.PI * radius * radius
}

class Rectangle(val width: Double, val height: Double) : Shape() {
    override fun calculateArea(): Double = width * height
}
```

The abstract class Shape defines the method calculatedArea, which is implemented by subclasses.

kotlin

```kotlin
val shapes: List<Shape> = listOf(Circle(5.0), Rectangle(4.0, 6.0))
shapes.forEach { println(it.calculateArea()) }
```

The list of shapes is processed uniformly, regardless of the specific type of each object.

Popular Design Patterns Implemented in Kotlin

Singleton

The Singleton pattern guarantees that a class has only a single instance. In Kotlin, this is implemented with the object object.

kotlin

```kotlin
object DatabaseConnection {
    fun connect() {
        println("Connected to the database.")
    }
```

```
}
```

The instance is automatically created the first time it is accessed.

kotlin

```
DatabaseConnection.connect()
```

Factory

The Factory pattern creates objects without exposing the creation process.

kotlin

```kotlin
class ShapeFactory {
    companion object {
        fun createShape(type: String): Shape {
            return when (type) {
                "circle" -> Circle(5.0)
                "rectangle" -> Rectangle(4.0, 6.0)
                else -> throw IllegalArgumentException("Unknown
shape type")
            }
        }
    }
}
```

The method createShape returns different implementations of Shape based on the type provided.

kotlin

```kotlin
val circle = ShapeFactory.createShape("circle")
println(circle.calculateArea())
```

Strategy

The Strategy pattern defines a family of algorithms and allows them to be interchangeable.

kotlin

```kotlin
interface PaymentStrategy {
    fun pay(amount: Double)
}

class CreditCardPayment : PaymentStrategy {
    override fun pay(amount: Double) {
        println("Paid $amount with credit card.")
    }
}

class PayPalPayment : PaymentStrategy {
    override fun pay(amount: Double) {
        println("Paid $amount via PayPal.")
    }
}
```

A interface PaymentStrategy **defines the contract for different payment strategies.**

kotlin

```kotlin
fun processPayment(amount: Double, strategy:
PaymentStrategy) {
    strategy.pay(amount)
}

val paymentMethod = CreditCardPayment()
processPayment(100.0, paymentMethod)
```

The method processPayment **accepts different implementations of** PaymentStrategy, **promoting flexibility.**

Observer

The Observer pattern defines a one-to-many dependency between objects, automatically notifying observers when state changes.

kotlin

```kotlin
class Subject {
    private val observers = mutableListOf<Observer>()

    fun addObserver(observer: Observer) {
        observers.add(observer)
    }

    fun notifyObservers() {
        observers.forEach { it.update() }
    }
}

interface Observer {
    fun update()
}

class ConcreteObserver : Observer {
    override fun update() {
        println("Observer notified.")
    }
}
```

The class Subject manages the observers, while each observer implements the interface Observer.

kotlin

```kotlin
val subject = Subject()
val observer = ConcreteObserver()
subject.addObserver(observer)
subject.notifyObservers()
```

Observers are automatically notified when the subject's state changes.

Kotlin offers robust tools to implement fundamental Object-Oriented Programming concepts, such as encapsulation, inheritance, and polymorphism, efficiently and expressively. Plus, its modern syntax makes it easy to adopt popular design patterns like Singleton, Factory, Strategy, and Observer. Mastering these concepts and practices is essential to creating well-designed, scalable, and easy-to-maintain systems.

CHAPTER 14: FUNCTIONAL PROGRAMMING

Functional programming (FP) is a paradigm that treats functions as first-class citizens, allowing them to be passed as parameters, returned as values, and stored in variables. Kotlin combines functional and object-oriented programming principles, becoming a hybrid language that promotes expressiveness, modularity and ease of maintenance.

Functional Programming Principles in Kotlin

Functional programming is based on fundamental concepts that include **immutability**, **pure functions**, **function composition** and **lazy evaluation**.

Immutability

Immutability is a central principle in functional programming. In Kotlin, the use of immutable variables is encouraged (val) and immutable collections to avoid side effects.

kotlin

```
val numbers = listOf(1, 2, 3, 4, 5)
val squaredNumbers = numbers.map { it * it }
println(squaredNumbers) // Exibe [1, 4, 9, 16, 25]
```

The use of val and the transformation of the list with map ensure that none of the collections are modified.

Pure Functions

A pure function is one whose result depends only on the given arguments, without changing the external state or producing side effects.

kotlin

```kotlin
fun add(a: Int, b: Int): Int {
    return a + b
}
```

This function always returns the same result for the same arguments and does not change any variables outside its scope.

Function Composition

Composition allows you to combine smaller functions into larger functions, promoting code reuse.

kotlin

```kotlin
fun double(x: Int) = x * 2
fun square(x: Int) = x * x

fun composeAndApply(x: Int): Int {
    return square(double(x))
}

println(composeAndApply(3)) // Displays 36
```

Smaller functions are combined to perform more complex calculations.

Lazy Evaluation

Lazy evaluation processes values only when necessary, saving resources and improving performance.

kotlin

```kotlin
val sequence = generateSequence(1) { it + 1 }
val firstTenSquares = sequence.map { it * it }.take(10).toList()
println(firstTenSquares) // Displays [1, 4, 9, 16, 25, 36, 49, 64, 81, 100]
```

Numbers are generated and processed on demand, avoiding excessive memory usage.

Using Functions as First-Class Objects

Functions in Kotlin can be assigned to variables, passed as parameters, and returned from other functions.

Higher Order Functions

Higher-order functions accept other functions as parameters or return functions.

kotlin

```kotlin
fun calculate(a: Int, b: Int, operation: (Int, Int) -> Int): Int {
    return operation(a, b)
}

val sum = calculate(4, 5) { x, y -> x + y }
val product = calculate(4, 5) { x, y -> x * y }
println(sum) // Displays 9
println(product) // Exibe 20
```

The function calculate applies different operations based on the function provided as an argument.

Lambdas

Lambdas are anonymous functions with a concise syntax.

kotlin

```kotlin
val square: (Int) -> Int = { it * it }
println(square(6)) // Displays 36
```

The operator it represents the only argument of the lambda.

Named Functions and Function References

Functions can be used directly as values with function

references.

kotlin

```
fun multiplyByThree(x: Int): Int = x * 3

val operation = ::multiplyByThree
println(operation(5)) // Displays 15
```

The reference ::multiplyByThree assigns the function multiplyByThree to a variable.

Returning Functions

Functions can return other functions.

kotlin

```
fun createMultiplier(factor: Int): (Int) -> Int {
    return { x -> x * factor }
}

val multiplyByTwo = createMultiplier(2)
println(multiplyByTwo(5)) // Displays 10
```

The method createMultiplier returns a lambda that multiplies by the given factor.

Manipulating Collections with Functional Operations

Kotlin offers a rich collections API with functional operations like map, filter, reduce and groupBy.

Transformation with map

The method map applies a transformation to each element in a collection.

kotlin

```
val numbers = listOf(1, 2, 3, 4, 5)
val doubled = numbers.map { it * 2 }
println(doubled) // Exibe [2, 4, 6, 8, 10]
```

Each number is multiplied by 2, resulting in a new list.

Filtering with filter

The method filter selects elements that meet a condition.

kotlin

```
val evenNumbers = numbers.filter { it % 2 == 0 }
println(evenNumbers) // Displays [2, 4]
```

The condition it % 2 == 0 ensures that only even numbers are included.

Aggregation with reduce

The method reduce combines elements from a collection into a single value.

kotlin

```
val sum = numbers.reduce { acc, num -> acc + num }
println(sum) // Displays 15
```

The accumulator (acc) adds each element in the list.

Grouping with groupBy

The method groupBy organizes elements into subcollections based on a key.

kotlin

```
val words = listOf("apple", "banana", "cherry", "date")
val groupedByLength = words.groupBy { it.length }
println(groupedByLength) // Displays {5=[apple], 6=[banana,
cherry], 4=[date]}
```

Words are grouped by length.

Ordering with sortedBy

The method sortedBy Orders elements based on a criterion.

kotlin

```
val sorted = numbers.sortedByDescending { it }
println(sorted) // Displays [5, 4, 3, 2, 1]
```

The numbers are sorted in descending order.

Lazy Processing with Sequences

Sequences are ideal for large collections or chained operations.

kotlin

```
val lazySequence = numbers.asSequence().filter { it % 2 ==
0 }.map { it * it }
println(lazySequence.toList()) // Exibe [4, 16]
```

The operations filter and map are performed only when necessary.

Combining Functional Operations

Functional operations can be combined to perform complex transformations.

kotlin

```
val results = numbers
    .filter { it % 2 != 0 }
    .map { it * it }
    .sortedByDescending { it }
println(results) // Displays [25, 9, 1]
```

The list is filtered to include only odd numbers, the remaining elements are squared and sorted in descending order.

Good Practices in Functional Programming

1. Prefer Immutability Whenever Possible

Use immutable variables and collections to avoid unwanted side effects.

2. **Use Pure Functions**
   Reduce dependency on external state for easier testing and maintenance.

3. **Avoid Imperative Loops**
   Replace traditional loops with functional operations to improve code clarity.

kotlin

```kotlin
val total = (1..10).sum()
println(total) // Displays 55
```

4. **Take advantage of Lazy Assessment**
   Use sequences to process large volumes of data efficiently.

5. **Break down complex functions into smaller ones**
   Separate logic into reusable functions to improve readability.

Functional programming in Kotlin offers powerful tools for creating more expressive, modular, and efficient code. By using functions as first-class objects and manipulating collections through functional operations, you can implement elegant and robust solutions. Applying best practices ensures that code is clear, predictable and easy to maintain, promoting more productive development.

CHAPTER 15: ASYNCHRONOUS PROGRAMMING

Asynchronous programming is essential for creating responsive and efficient applications, especially in scenarios that involve input/output (I/O) operations, such as network calls, reading files, and interactions with databases. Kotlin introduces coroutines as a powerful solution to handle concurrency and asynchronous tasks in a simpler and more readable way.

Working with Coroutines in Kotlin

Coroutines are a lightweight and efficient way to manage asynchronous tasks in Kotlin. They are performed in **corrotina contexts**, which can be system threads or optimized thread pools.

Introduction to suspend

The modifier suspend is used to declare functions that can be paused and resumed. A function marked as suspend can only be called within another coroutine or a higher-order function such as runBlocking.

kotlin

```kotlin
suspend fun fetchData(): String {
    // Simulates a long-running operation
    return "Data fetched"
}
```

This function simulates an operation that can be suspended and resumed without blocking the thread.

Creating Coroutines

The function launch is used to start a coroutine. It is provided by the library kotlinx.coroutines, which must be added to the project.

kotlin

```kotlin
import kotlinx.coroutines.*

fun main() = runBlocking {
    launch {
        println("Starting coroutine...")
        delay(1000L) // Suspend execution for 1 second
        println("Coroutine finished.")
    }
    println("RunBlocking finished.")
}
```

In the example, the function delay suspends coroutine execution for 1 second, allowing other coroutines to run during that time.

Scope of Coroutines

THE **coroutine scope** determines the lifecycle of coroutines. THE CoroutineScope is a tool for managing scope.

kotlin

```kotlin
fun main() = runBlocking {
    val scope = CoroutineScope(Dispatchers.Default)
    scope.launch {
        println("Running in custom scope")
    }
}
```

THE CoroutineScope uses Dispatchers.Default to run coroutines on an optimized thread pool.

Coroutine Builders

launch

Starts a coroutine that returns no results.

kotlin

```kotlin
launch {
    println("Launch coroutine")
}
```

async

Starts a coroutine that returns a value encapsulated in a Deferred.

kotlin

```kotlin
val deferred = async {
    "Result from async"
}
println(deferred.await())
```

runBlocking

Blocks the main thread until all coroutines in its scope complete.

kotlin

```kotlin
runBlocking {
    println("RunBlocking executed")
}
```

delay vs Thread.sleep

The method delay suspends the coroutine without blocking the thread, while Thread.sleep blocks the entire thread.

kotlin

```kotlin
launch {
    println("Coroutine started")
    delay(1000L)
```

```
    println("Coroutine resumed")
}
```

To use delay It is more efficient in applications with multiple simultaneous tasks.

Async, Await and Concurrency Management

Using async and await

The function async allows you to launch asynchronous tasks that return a result. The method await retrieves this result.

kotlin

```
suspend fun fetchUser(): String {
    delay(1000L) // Simulates an API call
    return "User data"
}

suspend fun fetchPosts(): String {
    delay(1000L) // Simulate another API call
    return "Posts data"
}

fun main() = runBlocking {
    val userDeferred = async { fetchUser() }
    val postsDeferred = async { fetchPosts() }

    println("Fetching data...")
    println(userDeferred.await()) // Wait for the result of
fetchUser
    println(postsDeferred.await()) // Waiting for the result of
fetchPosts
}
```

Two tasks are executed simultaneously, saving time compared to sequential execution.

Managing Competition with Dispatcher

You **dispatchers** define the execution context of coroutines.

- Dispatchers.Default: **Pool of threads optimized for CPU-intensive tasks.**
- Dispatchers.IO: **Optimized for I/O operations such as reading/writing files.**
- Dispatchers.Main: **Used to update the user interface in Android applications.**

kotlin

```
launch(Dispatchers.IO) {
    println("Running on IO dispatcher")
}
```

Coroutines can switch between dispatchers to optimize execution.

Structure withContext

The function withContext changes the dispatcher of a coroutine without creating a new one.

kotlin

```
suspend fun readFile(): String = withContext(Dispatchers.IO) {
    delay(500L) // Simulates file reading
    "File content"
}

fun main() = runBlocking {
    val content = readFile()
    println(content)
}
```

This approach is useful for performing specific operations in different contexts.

Practical Examples to Simplify Asynchronous Tasks

Parallelism in Data Processing

Coroutines can be used to process large volumes of data simultaneously.

kotlin

```kotlin
suspend fun processChunk(data: List<Int>): Int {
    delay(500L) // Simulates processing
    return data.sum()
}

fun main() = runBlocking {
    val data = (1..100).toList()
    val chunks = data.chunked(25)

    val results = chunks.map { chunk ->
        async { processChunk(chunk) }
    }

    val totalSum = results.sumOf { it.await() }
    println("Total Sum: $totalSum")
}
```

The dataset is divided into smaller parts, processed in parallel, and the results are combined.

Timeout com withTimeout

Coroutines can automatically terminate if they exceed a time limit.

kotlin

```kotlin
suspend fun longRunningTask() {
    delay(2000L) // Simulates a long task
    println("Task completed")
}

fun main() = runBlocking {
    try {
```

```kotlin
    withTimeout(1000L) {
        longRunningTask()
    }
} catch (e: TimeoutCancellationException) {
    println("Task timed out")
    }
}
```

If the task is not completed within 1 second, the exception TimeoutCancellationException will be released.

Error Handling in Coroutines

Errors in coroutines can be handled with blocks try-catch.

kotlin

```kotlin
suspend fun failingTask() {
    throw RuntimeException("Something went wrong")
}

fun main() = runBlocking {
    try {
        failingTask()
    } catch (e: Exception) {
        println("Caught exception: ${e.message}")
    }
}
```

The exception is caught and handled to prevent application failures.

Using Coroutines in Android Applications

In Android, coroutines are used for asynchronous operations like API calls or database updates.

kotlin

```kotlin
class MyViewModel : ViewModel() {
```

```
    private val viewModelScope =
CoroutineScope(Dispatchers.Main)

    fun fetchData() {
        viewModelScope.launch {
            val data = withContext(Dispatchers.IO) {
                fetchFromApi() // Simulates API call
            }
            updateUI(data) // Updates the user interface
        }
    }
}
```

THE viewModelScope ensures that coroutines are automatically canceled at the end of the ViewModel's lifecycle.

Good Practices in Asynchronous Programming

1. **Choose the Right Dispatcher**
   Use Dispatchers.Default for CPU, Dispatchers.IO for I/O and Dispatchers.Main for UI.
2. **Evite Bloquear Threads**
   Replace Thread.sleep by delay so as not to block execution.
3. **Manage the Scope of Coroutines**
   Use scopes like CoroutineScope or viewModelScope to control the lifecycle of coroutines.
4. **Handle Exceptions with SupervisorJob**
   Use SupervisorJob to isolate failures and prevent one coroutine from canceling others.
5. **Divide Tasks into Suspend Functions**
   Break complex tasks into small, reusable functions to improve readability.

Asynchronous programming with coroutines in Kotlin simplifies complex tasks, promoting efficiency and clarity. With tools like async, await, launch and withContext, it is possible to manage competition robustly. Applying best practices ensures that code is reliable, responsive, and prepared to handle concurrent operations in different contexts.

CHAPTER 16: INTEGRATION WITH APIS

Integrating with APIs is a common task in modern application development. REST APIs provide a standardized way to access remote resources, such as data from a server or external services. In Kotlin, libraries like Retrofit and Ktor simplify interaction with APIs, while tools for JSON processing make response management more efficient and intuitive.

Consumindo APIs REST no Kotlin

REST APIs use HTTP methods, such as GET, POST, PUT, and DELETE, to access or modify resources. Working with REST APIs involves sending HTTP requests and processing the responses.

Creating a Basic HTTP Request

The Java standard library can be used to perform simple HTTP requests.

kotlin

```kotlin
import java.net.HttpURLConnection
import java.net.URL

fun fetchApiData(url: String): String {
    val connection = URL(url).openConnection() as
HttpURLConnection
    return try {
        connection.inputStream.bufferedReader().use
{ it.readText() }
    } finally {
        connection.disconnect()
    }
```

```
}
fun main() {
   val data = fetchApiData("https://
jsonplaceholder.typicode.com/posts/1")
   println(data)
}
```

The method fetchApiData performs a GET request and returns the response as a string. However, this method is basic and can be complex for more advanced tasks such as dealing with headers or authentication.

Working with Retrofit

Retrofit is a popular library for consuming REST APIs. It simplifies managing HTTP requests and processing responses.

Retrofit Configuration

Add the Retrofit dependency to your file build.gradle.

groovy

```
implementation 'com.squareup.retrofit2:retrofit:2.9.0'
implementation 'com.squareup.retrofit2:converter-gson:2.9.0'
```

THE converter-gson is used to automatically convert JSON responses into Kotlin objects.

Creating the Retrofit Client

Define an interface to map the API endpoints.

kotlin

```
import retrofit2.Call
import retrofit2.http.GET
import retrofit2.http.Path

interface ApiService {
   @GET("posts/{id}")
```

```kotlin
    fun getPost(@Path("id") id: Int): Call<Post>
}
```

O endpoint posts/{id} is configured with the method GET. The parameter id is passed as part of the URL.

Defining the Data Model

Create a data class to represent the API response.

kotlin

```kotlin
data class Post(
    val userId: Int,
    val id: Int,
    val title: String,
    val body: String
)
```

Initializing the Retrofit

Configure the Retrofit client with the API base URL.

kotlin

```kotlin
import retrofit2.Retrofit
import retrofit2.converter.gson.GsonConverterFactory

val retrofit = Retrofit.Builder()
    .baseUrl("https://jsonplaceholder.typicode.com/")
    .addConverterFactory(GsonConverterFactory.create())
    .build()

val apiService = retrofit.create(ApiService::class.java)
```

The method addConverterFactory configures Retrofit to use Gson as a JSON converter.

Consuming the API

Make the call and process the response.

kotlin

```kotlin
import retrofit2.Call
import retrofit2.Callback
import retrofit2.Response

fun main() {
    val call = apiService.getPost(1)
    call.enqueue(object : Callback<Post> {
        override fun onResponse(call: Call<Post>, response:
Response<Post>) {
            if (response.isSuccessful) {
                val post = response.body()
                println("Title: ${post?.title}")
            } else {
                println("Request failed with code: $
{response.code()}")
            }
        }

        override fun onFailure(call: Call<Post>, t: Throwable) {
            println("Error: ${t.message}")
        }
    })
}
```

The method enqueue executes the request in a separate thread, avoiding blocking the UI.

Working with Ktor

Ktor is a modern and flexible library for creating and consuming APIs. It supports both clients and servers.

Ktor Configuration

Add dependencies to the file build.gradle.

groovy

```
implementation "io.ktor:ktor-client-core:2.0.0"
implementation "io.ktor:ktor-client-cio:2.0.0"
implementation "io.ktor:ktor-client-content-negotiation:2.0.0"
implementation "io.ktor:ktor-serialization-gson:2.0.0"
```

Criando o Cliente Ktor

Configure the HTTP client.

kotlin

```kotlin
import io.ktor.client.*
import io.ktor.client.call.*
import io.ktor.client.plugins.contentnegotiation.*
import io.ktor.client.request.*
import io.ktor.serialization.gson.*

val client = HttpClient {
    install(ContentNegotiation) {
        gson()
    }
}
```

O plugin ContentNegotiation configures the client to automatically convert JSON responses.

Consumindo uma API com Ktor

Make a GET request and process the response.

kotlin

```kotlin
suspend fun fetchPost(id: Int): Post {
    return client.get("https://jsonplaceholder.typicode.com/
posts/$id").body()
}

fun main() = kotlinx.coroutines.runBlocking {
    val post = fetchPost(1)
    println("Title: ${post.title}")
```

```
}
```

The method body converts the JSON response into a Kotlin object.

Dealing with Headers and Parameters

Add headers or parameters to the request.

kotlin

```
suspend fun fetchWithHeaders(id: Int): Post {
    return client.get("https://jsonplaceholder.typicode.com/
posts/$id") {
        headers {
            append("Authorization", "Bearer your_token")
        }
    }.body()
}
```

Headers are configured within the block headers.

Processing JSON Responses

Converting JSON to Kotlin objects is a common task when consuming APIs. Tools like Gson and Kotlin Serialization make this process easy.

Using Gson

Gson is a popular library for manipulating JSON.

kotlin

```
import com.google.gson.Gson

val json = """
    {
        "userId": 1,
        "id": 1,
        "title": "Post title",
```

```
        "body": "Post body"
    }
"""

val gson = Gson()
val post = gson.fromJson(json, Post::class.java)
println(post.title) // Exibe "Post title"
```

The method fromJson converts a JSON string to a Kotlin object.

Usando Kotlin Serialization

Kotlin Serialization is built into the language and supports serialization and deserialization.

Add the necessary dependencies.

groovy

```
implementation "org.jetbrains.kotlinx:kotlinx-serialization-json:1.3.3"
```

Note the data class with @Serializable.

kotlin

```
import kotlinx.serialization.Serializable
import kotlinx.serialization.json.Json

@Serializable
data class Post(
    val userId: Int,
    val id: Int,
    val title: String,
    val body: String
)

val json = """
    {
        "userId": 1,
        "id": 1,
```

```
    "title": "Post title",
    "body": "Post body"
  }
"""
```

```
val post = Json.decodeFromString<Post>(json)
println(post.title) // Exibe "Post title"
```

The method decodeFromString converts the JSON to an instance of the data class.

Validating and Handling Errors in Responses

Check the status code and handle errors accordingly.

kotlin

```
fun handleApiResponse(response: Response<Post>) {
  if (response.isSuccessful) {
    println("Data: ${response.body()?.title}")
  } else {
    println("Error: ${response.code()}")
  }
}
```

Responses with non-2xx status codes are handled separately.

Good Practices

1. **Use Libraries**
   Prefer Retrofit or Ktor to simplify API consumption and automatically handle headers, errors, and JSON conversions.
2. **Validate Answers**
   Always validate HTTP status codes before processing data.
3. **Implement Cache**
   To reduce redundant calls, implement caching where necessary.

4. **Manage Errors**
   Handle exceptions to avoid unexpected failures.

5. **Prefer Data Classes**
   Use data classes to map JSON responses, ensuring consistency and type safety.

6. **Use Asynchronous Operations**
   Perform API calls in coroutines to avoid blocking the UI.

Integration with REST APIs in Kotlin is simplified by tools like Retrofit and Ktor. Converting JSON responses to Kotlin objects is made easy by libraries like Gson and Kotlin Serialization. Following good practices for validation, error handling, and asynchronous operations ensures that consuming APIs is efficient, secure, and scalable.

CHAPTER 17: DATA PERSISTENCE

Persisting data is an essential part of developing applications that need to store information in a lasting way. In Kotlin, frameworks like SQLite and Room simplify database management by offering modern, secure tools for handling local persistence. This chapter explores how to work with databases, configure and perform basic queries using object-relational mapping (ORM) frameworks.

Working with Databases in Kotlin

Fundamental Concepts

Relational databases store data in tables, where each table is made up of rows and columns. To interact with these banks, languages such as SQL (Structured Query Language) are used. In Kotlin, frameworks like SQLite and Room abstract much of the manual work, making data persistence more efficient and readable.

Introduction to SQLite

SQLite is a lightweight database, integrated into most operating systems and ideal for local persistence in Android applications.

SQLite Configuration on Android

To use SQLite in an Android application, create a subclass of SQLiteOpenHelper. This class manages database creation and updating.

kotlin

```
import android.content.Context
import android.database.sqlite.SQLiteDatabase
```

```
import android.database.sqlite.SQLiteOpenHelper

class DatabaseHelper(context: Context) :
SQLiteOpenHelper(context, "my_database.db", null, 1) {

    override fun onCreate(db: SQLiteDatabase) {
        db.execSQL("""
            CREATE TABLE users (
                id INTEGER PRIMARY KEY AUTOINCREMENT,
                name TEXT NOT NULL,
                age INTEGER NOT NULL
            )
        """)
    }

    override fun onUpgrade(db: SQLiteDatabase, oldVersion: Int,
newVersion: Int) {
        db.execSQL("DROP TABLE IF EXISTS users")
        onCreate(db)
    }
}
```

The method onCreate is called the first time the database is accessed, creating the table users.

Inserting Data into SQLite

To enter data, use the method insert of the class SQLiteDatabase.

kotlin

```
fun insertUser(dbHelper: DatabaseHelper, name: String, age:
Int) {
    val db = dbHelper.writableDatabase
    val values = ContentValues().apply {
        put("name", name)
        put("age", age)
    }
    db.insert("users", null, values)
```

```
}
```

The method ContentValues is used to map columns to values to be inserted.

kotlin

```
val dbHelper = DatabaseHelper(context)
insertUser(dbHelper, "Alice", 30)
```

Querying Data in SQLite

To recover data, use the method query.

kotlin

```
fun getUsers(dbHelper: DatabaseHelper): List<String> {
    val db = dbHelper.readableDatabase
    val cursor = db.query("users", arrayOf("name"), null, null,
null, null, null)
    val users = mutableListOf<String>()
    with(cursor) {
        while (moveToNext()) {
            val name =
getString(getColumnIndexOrThrow("name"))
            users.add(name)
        }
    }
    cursor.close()
    return users
}
```

The data is read using a cursor, which iterates over the query results.

Updating and Deleting Data

To update records, use the method update.

kotlin

```kotlin
fun updateUserAge(dbHelper: DatabaseHelper, name: String,
newAge: Int) {
    val db = dbHelper.writableDatabase
    val values = ContentValues().apply {
        put("age", newAge)
    }
    db.update("users", values, "name = ?", arrayOf(name))
}
```

To delete records, use the method delete.

kotlin

```kotlin
fun deleteUser(dbHelper: DatabaseHelper, name: String) {
    val db = dbHelper.writableDatabase
    db.delete("users", "name = ?", arrayOf(name))
}
```

Using Room for Local Persistence

Room is an official Android library that abstracts manual work with SQLite, making data persistence more efficient and secure.

Room Configuration

Add dependencies to the file build.gradle.

groovy

```groovy
implementation "androidx.room:room-runtime:2.4.0"
capt "androidx.room:room-compiler:2.4.0"
```

Enable code generation using the capt.

groovy

```groovy
apply plugin: 'kotlin-kapt'
```

Creating the Entity

Annotate a data class with @Entity to define a table.

kotlin

```
import androidx.room.Entity
import androidx.room.PrimaryKey

@Entity(tableName = "users")
data class User(
    @PrimaryKey(autoGenerate = true) val id: Int = 0,
    val name: String,
    val age: Int
)
```

The class User represents the table users in the database.

Defining the DAO

The DAO (Data Access Object) is an interface that contains methods for accessing the database.

kotlin

```
import androidx.room.Dao
import androidx.room.Insert
import androidx.room.Query

@Knife
interface UserDao {
    @Insert
    suspend fun insert(user: User)

    @Query("SELECT * FROM users")
    suspend fun getAllUsers(): List<User>

    @Query("DELETE FROM users WHERE name = :name")
    suspend fun deleteByName(name: String)
}
```

Methods are annotated to map SQL operations.

Creating the Database

Annotate an abstract class with @Database and extend RoomDatabase.

kotlin

```kotlin
import androidx.room.Database
import androidx.room.RoomDatabase

@Database(entities = [User::class], version = 1)
abstract class AppDatabase : RoomDatabase() {
    abstract fun userDao(): UserDao
}
```

Initialize the database using the Room builder.

kotlin

```kotlin
val db = Room.databaseBuilder(
    context,
    AppDatabase::class.java,
    "app_database"
).build()
val userDao = db.userDao()
```

Room Operations

Insert, query, and delete data using DAO functions.

kotlin

```kotlin
suspend fun performDatabaseOperations(userDao: UserDao) {
    userDao.insert(User(name = "Bob", age = 25))
    val users = userDao.getAllUsers()
    users.forEach { println("${it.name} - ${it.age}") }
    userDao.deleteByName("Bob")
}
```

Asynchronous operations use coroutines to avoid blocking in

the user interface.

Basic Configuration and Queries with ORM Frameworks

ORM (Object-Relational Mapping) frameworks map classes directly to tables in the database, eliminating the need to write SQL manually.

Advantages of ORM

- **Code Reduction**: Operations such as insertion and query are simplified.
- **Security**: Prevents SQL Injection attacks.
- **Maintenance**: Changes to the schema are reflected directly in the code.

Advanced Queries in Room

In addition to basic queries, Room supports complex queries.

kotlin

```
@Query("SELECT * FROM users WHERE age > :minAge ORDER BY name ASC")
suspend fun getUsersOlderThan(minAge: Int): List<User>
```

The query returns all users older than the given value, sorted by name.

kotlin

```
val olderUsers = userDao.getUsersOlderThan(20)
olderUsers.forEach { println(it.name) }
```

Relationships in Room

Room supports relationships between tables.

kotlin

```
@Entity
data class Order(
```

```
@PrimaryKey(autoGenerate = true) val id: Int = 0,
val userId: Int,
val amount: Double
)

data class UserWithOrders(
    @Embedded val user: User,
    @Relation(
        parentColumn = "id",
        entityColumn = "userId"
    )
    val orders: List<Order>
)

@Knife
interface UserOrderDao {
    @Transaction
    @Query("SELECT * FROM users WHERE id = :userId")
    suspend fun getUserWithOrders(userId: Int):
UserWithOrders
}
```

The methods annotated with @Relation automatically manage mapping between tables.

kotlin

```
val userWithOrders = userOrderDao.getUserWithOrders(1)
println(userWithOrders.orders)
```

Good Practices

1. **Use Room Whenever Possible**
   Prefer Room for local persistence in Android applications, taking advantage of its validations and code generation.
2. **Handle Exceptions**
   Always handle errors related to database operations to

avoid unexpected failures.

3. **Keep the Schema Updated**

   Perform migrations correctly when changing the database schema.

4. **Optimize Queries**

   Use optimized indexes and queries to improve performance.

5. **Manage Connections**

   Close SQLite connections appropriately to prevent memory leaks.

Persisting data locally is essential for many applications, and frameworks like SQLite and Room make this task practical and efficient. Room offers an additional level of abstraction and security, while SQLite provides granular control over the database. Applying best practices and understanding fundamental concepts ensures robust, high-performance integration with databases.

CHAPTER 18: AUTOMATED TESTING

Automated testing is an essential practice to ensure the quality, functionality and robustness of a system. They identify flaws in code before they reach the production environment, promoting confidence in ongoing development. In Kotlin, tools like JUnit and MockK offer complete support for creating and running unit and integration tests.

Creating Unit and Integration Tests in Kotlin

Difference between Unit and Integration Testing

- **Unit Tests**: Evaluate a single code unit, such as methods or functions, in isolation.
- **Integration Tests**: Validate the interaction between multiple units or components, ensuring that they work correctly together.

Test Environment Configuration

Add necessary dependencies to the file build.gradle.

groovy

```
dependencies {
    testImplementation "org.junit.jupiter:junit-jupiter:5.8.2"
    testImplementation "io.mockk:mockk:1.12.0"
}
```

Dependencies include JUnit for creating and running tests and MockK for creating mocks.

Structure of a Unit Test

Unit tests verify the behavior of individual functions or

methods. Use JUnit to define tests.

kotlin

```kotlin
import org.junit.jupiter.api.Assertions.*
import org.junit.jupiter.api.Test

class CalculatorTest {

    @Test
    fun `should add two numbers correctly`() {
        val result = add(2, 3)
        assertEquals(5, result)
    }

    private fun add(a: Int, b: Int): Int {
        return a + b
    }
}
```

The method assertEquals compares the expected value with the value returned by the function add.

Integration Tests

Integration tests verify that different parts of the system work together correctly.

kotlin

```kotlin
class UserRepository(private val database: Database) {
    fun getUser(id: Int): User? {
        return database.query("SELECT * FROM users WHERE id =
$id")
    }
}

class Database {
    fun query(sql: String): User? {
        // Simulates a database query
```

```kotlin
        return User(1, "Alice")
    }
}

class UserRepositoryTest {

    @Test
    fun `should fetch user from database`() {
        val database = Database()
        val repository = UserRepository(database)

        val user = repository.getUser(1)

        assertNotNull(user)
        assertEquals("Alice", user?.name)
    }
}

data class User(val id: Int, val name: String)
```

In this example, the test checks whether the method getUser interacts correctly with the simulated database.

Configuration and Use of Libraries such as JUnit and MockK

Introduction to JUnit

JUnit is a widely used library for creating and running automated tests. In Kotlin, JUnit 5 (also known as JUnit Jupiter) is the recommended version.

Structure of a Test with JUnit

Test methods are annotated with @Test.

kotlin

```kotlin
import org.junit.jupiter.api.Assertions.*
import org.junit.jupiter.api.Test

class StringUtilsTest {
```

```kotlin
@Test
fun `should reverse a string correctly`() {
    val reversed = reverseString("Kotlin")
    assertEquals("niltok", reversed)
}

private fun reverseString(input: String): String {
    return input.reversed()
}
}
```

Assertion methods, such as assertEquals, they check whether the expected result corresponds to the real one.

Configuring Tests with @BeforeEach and @AfterEach

Use notes @BeforeEach and @AfterEach to configure and clean up resources before and after each test.

kotlin

```kotlin
import org.junit.jupiter.api.BeforeEach
import org.junit.jupiter.api.AfterEach
import org.junit.jupiter.api.Test

class LifecycleTest {

    private var resource: String = ""

    @BeforeEach
    fun setUp() {
        resource = "Initialized"
    }

    @AfterEach
    fun tearDown() {
        resource = ""
    }

    @Test
```

```kotlin
fun `should use initialized resource`() {
    assertEquals("Initialized", resource)
}
}
```

Introduction to MockK

MockK is a powerful library for creating mocks, especially useful in tests that depend on external services or complex interactions.

Creating Mocks

Mocks are simulated instances of objects, used to replace real dependencies.

kotlin

```kotlin
import io.mock.*
import org.junit.jupiter.api.Test

class PaymentServiceTest {

    @Test
    fun `should process payment correctly`() {
        val paymentGateway = mockk<PaymentGateway>()
        every { paymentGateway.charge(any(), any()) } returns
true

        val service = PaymentService(paymentGateway)
        val result = service.processPayment(100.0)

        assertTrue(result)
        verify { paymentGateway.charge(100.0, "USD") }
    }
}

interface PaymentGateway {
    fun charge(amount: Double, currency: String): Boolean
}
```

```kotlin
class PaymentService(private val gateway: PaymentGateway) {
    fun processPayment(amount: Double): Boolean {
        return gateway.charge(amount, "USD")
    }
}
```

The method every defines the simulated behavior of the mock, while verify checks whether expected methods have been called.

Mocks with Dynamic Behavior

Mocks can return dynamic values based on arguments.

kotlin

```kotlin
every { paymentGateway.charge(less(50.0), any()) } returns false
every { paymentGateway.charge(greater(50.0), any()) } returns true
```

The methods less and greater allow you to define behavior based on conditions.

Capturing Arguments

MockK allows you to capture arguments to validate calls.

kotlin

```kotlin
val slot = slot<Double>()
every { paymentGateway.charge(capture(slot), any()) } returns true

service.processPayment(200.0)
assertEquals(200.0, slot.captured)
```

The captured value is stored in the slot for later checks.

Best Practices for Ensuring Code Quality

1. **Write Small, Isolated Tests**
   Make sure each test only checks a specific

functionality.

2. **Use Mocks Only When Necessary**
   Use mocks to replace external dependencies, but prefer
   to test real features whenever possible.

3. **Name Tests Clearly**
   Use descriptive names for test methods, indicating
   expected behavior.

kotlin

```kotlin
@Test
fun `should return error when input is invalid`() {
    // Clear and self-explanatory test
}
```

4. **Avoid Relying on Test Order**
   Tests must be independent, ensuring that they can be
   executed in any order.

5. **Adopt Code Coverage as a Metric**
   Monitor test coverage, but don't rely on it alone.
   Combine it with manual code reviews and analysis.

6. **Test Edge Cases**
   Ensure tests cover extreme inputs or unexpected
   conditions.

kotlin

```kotlin
@Test
fun `should handle empty input gracefully`() {
    val result = processInput("")
    assertEquals("No data", result)
}
```

7. **Integre Testes no Pipeline CI/CD**
   Automate test execution in continuous integration
   and delivery pipelines.

8. **Use Integration Tests for Critical Components**

Validate interactions between services or modules to avoid integration failures.

kotlin

```
@Test
fun `should save user and fetch it correctly`() {
    repository.save(User(1, "Alice"))
    val user = repository.findById(1)
    assertNotNull(user)
    assertEquals("Alice", user?.name)
}
```

Automated tests are essential to guarantee the quality and reliability of systems under development. With tools like JUnit and MockK, you can create clear and efficient tests, covering everything from individual functions to complex interactions between components. Applying good practices in test development and maintenance results in more robust code, reducing failures and facilitating system evolution over time.

CHAPTER 19: WORKING WITH KOTLIN MULTIPLATFORM

Kotlin Multiplatform is a powerful technology that allows you to share code across different platforms, including Android, iOS, backend, and web. This approach reduces code duplication and improves efficiency in developing applications that need to serve multiple ecosystems. This chapter covers the fundamental concepts of Kotlin Multiplatform, how to configure it and use it to create projects that share code between different platforms.

What is Kotlin Multiplatform

Kotlin Multiplatform (KMP) is a feature of Kotlin that allows you to write common code that can be shared across platforms, while allowing you to implement functionality specific to each of them. It is designed to combine the flexibility of code sharing with the ability to access platform-specific APIs.

Main Features

- **Shared Code**: Allows you to share business logic, validations, data models and algorithms between different platforms.
- **Platform-Specific Code**: Supports the implementation of specific functionalities using native code.
- **Ecosystem Compatibility**: Works with Android, iOS, JVM, JavaScript, WebAssembly and more.

Benefits

- **Effort Reduction**: Eliminates the need to duplicate business logic in different languages.
- **Flexibility**: Does not force the use of a single framework,

allowing integration with existing projects.

- **Simplified Maintenance**: Centralizes business logic, facilitating updates and bug fixes.

Setup and Getting Started

Setting Up a Multiplatform Kotlin Project

Prerequisites

Before you begin, make sure you have the following tools installed:

- **Kotlin 1.5 or higher**
- **I understand the idea** (Community or Ultimate version) or Android Studio
- **Gradle 7.0 or higher**

Creating the Project

1. Open IntelliJ IDEA or Android Studio.
2. Choice **New Project** and select **Kotlin Multiplatform**.
3. Configure the project name, directory and language (Kotlin).

The project created will contain a basic structure with separate modules for shared code and specific ones for each platform.

Project Structure

The typical structure of a Kotlin Multiplatform project includes:

- **shared/**: Contains code shared across platforms.
- **androidApp/**: Contains Android specific code.
- **iosApp/**: Contains iOS-specific code.

Configuring the Build Script

Update the file build.gradle.kts in the shared module to include the cross-platform targets.

kotlin

plugins {

```
    kotlin("multiplatform")
}
kotlin {
    android()
    ios()
    jvm()

    sourceSets {
        val commonMain by getting {
            dependencies {
                implementation(kotlin("stdlib"))
            }
        }
        val androidMain by getting
        val iosMain by getting
    }
}
```

This script configures targets for Android, iOS and JVM, as well as defining shared code in commonMain.

Writing Shared Code

No module shared, create the logic that will be shared across platforms.

kotlin

```
// shared/src/commonMain/kotlin/Utils.kt
fun greet(name: String): String {
    return "Hello, $name!"
}
```

This code will be available for all platforms configured in the project.

Implementing Platform-Specific Code

If a feature needs to access platform-specific APIs, use the keyword expect to define the interface in the shared code and actual to implement it on each platform.

Shared Code

kotlin

```
// shared/src/commonMain/kotlin/Platform.kt
expect fun getPlatformName(): String
```

Android Code

kotlin

```
// shared/src/androidMain/kotlin/Platform.kt
actual fun getPlatformName(): String {
    return "Android"
}
```

iOS Code

kotlin

```
// shared/src/iosMain/kotlin/Platform.kt
import platform.UIKit.UIDevice

actual fun getPlatformName(): String {
    return UIDevice.currentDevice.systemName() + " " +
UIDevice.currentDevice.systemVersion
}
```

This approach ensures that shared code can call getPlatformName() without knowing details of specific implementations.

Integration with Android and iOS Applications

Android

Add the shared module as a dependency in the file build.gradle of the Android app.

groovy

```
dependencies {
    implementation(project(":shared"))
}
```

Use functions from shared code in the Android project.

kotlin

```kotlin
class MainActivity : AppCompatActivity() {
    override fun onCreate(savedInstanceState: Bundle?) {
        super.onCreate(savedInstanceState)
        val message = greet("Android")
        println(message)
    }
}
```

iOS

Integrate the shared module into the Xcode project using the framework generated by Kotlin Multiplatform.

1. Configure the build task in build.gradle.kts to generate the iOS framework.

kotlin

```kotlin
kotlin {
    ios {
        binaries {
            framework {
                baseName = "SharedCode"
            }
        }
    }
}
```

2. In Xcode, import the generated framework and use the shared functions.

swift

```
import SharedCode

let message = SharedCodeKt.greet(name: "iOS")
print(message)
```

Sharing Code between Android, iOS and Backend

Kotlin Multiplatform also allows you to share code between the frontend and backend. This is useful for validating business rules or sharing data models.

Sharing Data Models

Define the data models in the shared module.

kotlin

```
// shared/src/commonMain/kotlin/Models.kt
data class User(val id: Int, val name: String)
```

No backend (usando Ktor):

kotlin

```
// backend/src/main/kotlin/Server.kt
import io.ktor.application.*
import io.ktor.response.*
import io.ktor.routing.*
import io.ktor.server.engine.*
import io.ktor.server.netty.*

fun main() {
    embeddedServer(Netty, port = 8080) {
        routing {
            get("/user") {
                call.respond(User(1, "John Doe"))
            }
        }
```

```
}.start(wait = true)
}
```

On the frontend (Android/iOS), consume the API to access the same models.

Shared Validation

Implement validations in shared code.

kotlin

```
// shared/src/commonMain/kotlin/Validation.kt
fun validateName(name: String): Boolean {
    return name.isNotBlank() && name.length > 2
}
```

Use this logic on both the backend and frontend.

Good Practices

1. **Centralize Shared Logic**
   Focus business rules, validations, and models on shared code.
2. **Use Specific Implementations Sparingly**
   Implement specific code only when necessary, using expect and actual.
3. **Automatize Build e Testes**
   Configure CI/CD pipelines to build and test the project on all platforms.
4. **Keep the Code Modular**
   Separate functionalities into distinct modules to facilitate maintenance and scalability.
5. **Test on All Platforms**
   Ensure that the shared code works correctly on all configured platforms.

Kotlin Multiplatform offers an efficient solution for developing cross-platform applications, reducing code duplication and improving consistency between Android, iOS and backend. The flexibility of integrating shared and specific code allows you to build robust and scalable systems, while good practices guarantee an efficient and high-quality development flow.

CHAPTER 20: CREATING ANDROID APPLICATIONS WITH KOTLIN

Kotlin is the official language for Android development, offering concise syntax, security, and native support in Android Studio. Developing Android applications with Kotlin allows you to take advantage of modern language features and powerful platform tools. This chapter covers everything from getting started with Android development to the lifecycle of activities and fragments, as well as tips for creating dynamic user interfaces.

Introduction to Android Development with Kotlin

Android is a widely used operating system designed for mobile devices. Android applications are built using the Android SDK, which provides tools for accessing system components, creating user interfaces, and managing lifecycles.

Structure of an Android Project

When you create an Android project in Android Studio, the project structure is organized into:

- **app/**: Contains the source code and resources of the application.
- **res/**: Stores visuals, XML layouts, strings and other necessary files.
- **manifest/**: Contains the file AndroidManifest.xml, which defines essential information about the application, such as activities and permissions.
- **build.gradle**: Manages dependencies and build configurations.

Creating an Android Project with Kotlin

1. Open Android Studio and choose **New Project**.
2. Select the initial template, such as **Empty Activity**.
3. Choice **Kotlin** like language.
4. Configure the project name, package, and minimum SDK version.

After creation, Android Studio generates a basic project with a single activity.

First Activity in Kotlin

An activity is an essential component that manages the interface of an application.

kotlin

```kotlin
import android.os.Bundle
import androidx.appcompat.app.AppCompatActivity

class MainActivity : AppCompatActivity() {
    override fun onCreate(savedInstanceState: Bundle?) {
        super.onCreate(savedInstanceState)
        setContentView(R.layout.activity_main)
    }
}
```

The method onCreate is called when the activity is created, and the layout is defined with the method setContentView.

Configuring the XML Layout

Layouts are defined in XML files in the folder res/layout.

xml

```xml
<!-- res/layout/activity_main.xml -->
<LinearLayout
    xmlns:android="http://schemas.android.com/apk/res/android"
    android:layout_width="match_parent"
```

```
    android:layout_height="match_parent"
    android:orientation="vertical">

<TextView
    android:id="@+id/textView"
    android:layout_width="wrap_content"
    android:layout_height="wrap_content"
    android:text="Hello, Android!" />

<Button
    android:id="@+id/button"
    android:layout_width="wrap_content"
    android:layout_height="wrap_content"
    android:text="Click Me" />
</LinearLayout>
```

This layout displays text and a button arranged vertically.

Interacting with the Interface

Interface elements can be accessed in Kotlin code using their IDs.

kotlin

```kotlin
import android.os.Bundle
import android.widget.Button
import android.widget.TextView
import androidx.appcompat.app.AppCompatActivity

class MainActivity : AppCompatActivity() {
    override fun onCreate(savedInstanceState: Bundle?) {
        super.onCreate(savedInstanceState)
        setContentView(R.layout.activity_main)

        val textView = findViewById<TextView>(R.id.textView)
        val button = findViewById<Button>(R.id.button)

        button.setOnClickListener {
            textView.text = "Button clicked!"
```

```
        }
    }
}
```

When the button is clicked, the text displayed in the TextView is dynamically changed.

Activity and Fragment Lifecycle

Activity Life Cycle

The lifecycle of an activity is managed by Android to optimize resources and ensure a good user experience. The main methods are:

- **onCreate**: Initializes the activity.
- **onStart**: Makes the activity visible.
- **onResume**: Makes the activity interactive.
- **onPause**: Pauses the activity, freeing up resources.
- **onStop**: Makes the activity invisible.
- **onDestroy**: Ends the activity.

kotlin

```kotlin
class MainActivity : AppCompatActivity() {
    override fun onCreate(savedInstanceState: Bundle?) {
        super.onCreate(savedInstanceState)
        println("Activity created")
    }

    override fun onStart() {
        super.onStart()
        println("Activity started")
    }

    override fun onResume() {
        super.onResume()
        println("Activity resumed")
    }
```

```kotlin
    override fun onPause() {
        super.onPause()
        println("Activity paused")
    }

    override fun onStop() {
        super.onStop()
        println("Activity stopped")
    }

    override fun onDestroy() {
        super.onDestroy()
        println("Activity destroyed")
    }
}
```

The log displays the lifecycle states as the activity starts, pauses, and ends.

Fragment Life Cycle

Fragments are reusable components that represent parts of the user interface within an activity.

kotlin

```kotlin
import android.os.Bundle
import androidx.fragment.app.Fragment

class ExampleFragment :
Fragment(R.layout.fragment_example) {
    override fun onCreate(savedInstanceState: Bundle?) {
        super.onCreate(savedInstanceState)
        println("Fragment created")
    }

    override fun onStart() {
        super.onStart()
        println("Fragment started")
```

```
    }
}
```

Fragments are added to an activity dynamically or defined in the XML layout.

Managing Fragments

Add a fragment dynamically using the FragmentManager.

kotlin

```
val fragment = ExampleFragment()
supportFragmentManager.beginTransaction()
    .replace(R.id.fragment_container, fragment)
    .commit()
```

The fragment is replaced in the specified container.

Tips for Creating Dynamic User Interfaces

Using ViewBinding

THE ViewBinding simplifies access to interface elements, eliminating the need for findViewById.

Enabling the ViewBinding

Add the configuration in the file build.gradle.

groovy

```
android {
    viewBinding {
        enabled = true
    }
}
```

Using the ViewBinding

kotlin

```
import android.os.Bundle
```

```kotlin
import androidx.appcompat.app.AppCompatActivity
import com.example.app.databinding.ActivityMainBinding

class MainActivity : AppCompatActivity() {
    private lateinit var binding: ActivityMainBinding

    override fun onCreate(savedInstanceState: Bundle?) {
        super.onCreate(savedInstanceState)
        binding = ActivityMainBinding.inflate(layoutInflater)
        setContentView(binding.root)

        binding.button.setOnClickListener {
            binding.textView.text = "Hello with ViewBinding!"
        }
    }
}
```

Creating Responsive Layouts

Use `ConstraintLayout` to create flexible and responsive interfaces.

xml

```xml
<androidx.constraintlayout.widget.ConstraintLayout
    xmlns:android="http://schemas.android.com/apk/res/android"
    xmlns:app="http://schemas.android.com/apk/res-auto"
    android:layout_width="match_parent"
    android:layout_height="match_parent">

    <TextView
        android:id="@+id/textView"
        android:layout_width="0dp"
        android:layout_height="wrap_content"
        android:text="Centered Text"
        app:layout_constraintTop_toTopOf="parent"
        app:layout_constraintBottom_toBottomOf="parent"
        app:layout_constraintStart_toStartOf="parent"
```

```
    app:layout_constraintEnd_toEndOf="parent" />
</androidx.constraintlayout.widget.ConstraintLayout>
```

THE ConstraintLayout Positions the text in the center of the screen.

Adding Animations

Use animations to improve the user experience.

kotlin

```kotlin
import android.animation.ObjectAnimator
import android.os.Bundle
import android.widget.TextView
import androidx.appcompat.app.AppCompatActivity

class MainActivity : AppCompatActivity() {
    override fun onCreate(savedInstanceState: Bundle?) {
        super.onCreate(savedInstanceState)
        setContentView(R.layout.activity_main)

        val textView = findViewById<TextView>(R.id.textView)
        ObjectAnimator.ofFloat(textView, "translationX",
200f).apply {
            duration = 1000
            start()
        }
    }
}
```

The animation moves the TextView horizontally.

Using RecyclerView for Lists

Create dynamic lists with RecyclerView.

    1. Add the dependency:

groovy

```
implementation 'androidx.recyclerview:recyclerview:1.2.1'
```

2. Configure o layout XML:

xml

```xml
<androidx.recyclerview.widget.RecyclerView
    android:id="@+id/recyclerView"
    android:layout_width="match_parent"
    android:layout_height="match_parent" />
```

3. Create an adapter:

kotlin

```kotlin
class MyAdapter(private val data: List<String>) :
    RecyclerView.Adapter<MyAdapter.ViewHolder>() {

    class ViewHolder(view: View) :
RecyclerView.ViewHolder(view) {
        val textView: TextView =
view.findViewById(R.id.textView)
    }

    override fun onCreateViewHolder(parent: ViewGroup,
viewType: Int): ViewHolder {
        val view = LayoutInflater.from(parent.context)
            .inflate(R.layout.item_view, parent, false)
        return ViewHolder(view)
    }

    override fun onBindViewHolder(holder: ViewHolder,
position: Int) {
        holder.textView.text = data[position]
    }

    override fun getItemCount(): Int = data.size
}
```

4. **Configure a** RecyclerView:

kotlin

```
val                        recyclerView              =
findViewById<RecyclerView>(R.id.recyclerView)
recyclerView.layoutManager = LinearLayoutManager(this)
recyclerView.adapter = MyAdapter(listOf("Item 1", "Item 2",
"Item 3"))
```

Android development with Kotlin is efficient and intuitive, allowing you to create modern applications with less effort. Mastering the lifecycle of activities and fragments, along with creating dynamic interfaces, is critical to building responsive and robust applications. Following the best practices described ensures a productive and high-quality development flow.

CHAPTER 21: BUILDING BACKENDS WITH KOTLIN

Kotlin is a versatile language, which in addition to being widely used in Android development, also stands out in the backend. With the framework **Which**, backend development in Kotlin becomes simple, efficient and highly productive. This chapter explores the use of Ktor to create APIs, configure routes, middleware, implement authentication and manage databases in backend applications.

Introduction to Ktor for Backend Development

Ktor is an asynchronous framework developed by JetBrains, designed to create modern backend applications, RESTful APIs, and web servers. It supports extensibility, modularity, and a lightweight design, allowing you to create highly customizable solutions.

Por que Usar Which one?

- **Lightweight and Modular**: Allows you to add only the necessary modules, avoiding unnecessary overhead.
- **Coroutine Support**: Based on Kotlin coroutines, it offers superior performance for asynchronous operations.
- **Flexibility**: Easily integrates with popular libraries and tools such as Exposed for databases and JWT authentication.

Setting up a Ktor Project

Creating a Ktor Project

1. Open IntelliJ IDEA and choose **New Project**.
2. Select **Which** no template menu.

3. Configure project options such as name, location and basic dependencies (Netty, Routing and ContentNegotiation).

Important Dependencies

In the archive build.gradle.kts, configure the basic dependencies for a Ktor project.

kotlin

```
plugins {
    application
    kotlin("jvm") version "1.8.0"
}

dependencies {
    implementation("io.ktor:ktor-server-core:2.0.0")
    implementation("io.ktor:ktor-server-netty:2.0.0")
    implementation("io.ktor:ktor-server-content-
negotiation:2.0.0")
    implementation("io.ktor:ktor-serialization-gson:2.0.0")
}
```

These dependencies include Netty server support, serialization, and routing.

Configuring the Server

The entry point for the Ktor application is the file Application.kt. Configure the server with the following code:

kotlin

```
import io.ktor.server.engine.*
import io.ktor.server.netty.*
import io.ktor.application.*
import io.ktor.response.*
import io.ktor.routing.*

fun main() {
```

```
    embeddedServer(Netty, port = 8080) {
        module()
    }.start(wait = true)
}

fun Application.module() {
    routing {
        get("/") {
            call.respondText("Hello, Ktor!")
        }
    }
}
```

When starting the server and accessing http://localhost:8080, the message "Hello, Ktor!" will be displayed.

Configuring Routes

Routes are entry points to the backend application. Ktor provides the module Routing to define and manage routes.

Creating Basic Routes

Add the routing module to the application.

kotlin

```
fun Application.module() {
    routing {
        get("/greet") {
            call.respondText("Hello, World!")
        }

        post("/submit") {
            val data = call.receiveText()
            call.respondText("Data received: $data")
        }
    }
}
```

- **GET**: Route that returns a fixed message.
- **POST**: Route that receives data from the client and returns a response with the data sent.

Routes with Parameters

Routes can include parameters to process dynamic requests.

kotlin

```kotlin
routing {
    get("/user/{id}") {
        val id = call.parameters["id"]
        call.respondText("User ID: $id")
    }
}
```

When accessed with http://localhost:8080/user/123, the route returns "User ID: 123".

Nested Routes

Organize complex routes using nested routes.

kotlin

```kotlin
routing {
    route("/api") {
        get("/users") {
            call.respondText("List of users")
        }
        get("/products") {
            call.respondText("List of products")
        }
    }
}
```

Nested routes allow you to group related endpoints under a common prefix, such as /api.

Middlewares no Which

Middlewares are functions that process requests or responses before or after they reach routes.

Intercepting Requests

Use the feature intercept to process requests before they arrive on the route.

kotlin

```kotlin
install(Routing) {
    intercept(ApplicationCallPipeline.Features) {
        println("Request URI: ${call.request.uri}")
    }
}
```

This setting logs the URI of each request to the console.

Adding Custom Plugins

Create custom middleware to validate headers.

kotlin

```kotlin
install(Routing) {
    intercept(ApplicationCallPipeline.Features) {
        if (call.request.headers["Authorization"] == null) {
            call.respondText("Missing Authorization Header",
status = HttpStatusCode.Unauthorized)
            finish()
        }
    }
}
```

This middleware checks whether the authorization header is present and rejects invalid requests.

Implementing Authentication

Authentication is essential to protect sensitive routes. Ktor supports several methods, including token-based authentication (JWT).

Configuring JWT

Add the dependency for JWT authentication.

kotlin

```
dependencies {
    implementation("io.ktor:ktor-server-auth:2.0.0")
    implementation("io.ktor:ktor-server-auth-jwt:2.0.0")
}
```

Configure the authenticator in Application.kt.

kotlin

```
import com.auth0.jwt.JWT
import com.auth0.jwt.algorithms.Algorithm
import io.ktor.auth.*
import io.ktor.auth.jwt.*

fun Application.configureSecurity() {
    install(Authentication) {
        jwt {
            realm = "which sample app"
            verifier(
                JWT
                    .require(Algorithm.HMAC256("secret"))
                    .withIssuer("ktor.io")
                    .build()
            )
            validate { credential ->
                if (credential.payload.getClaim("name").asString() !=
null) JWTPrincipal(credential.payload) else null
            }
        }
```

```
    }
}
```

Securing Routes with Authentication

Add authentication to routes.

kotlin

```
fun Application.module() {
    configureSecurity()

    routing {
        authenticate {
            get("/secure") {
                call.respondText("You are authenticated!")
            }
        }
    }
}
```

Routes within the block authenticate require a valid JWT token.

Database Management in Backend Applications

Database management is crucial for backend applications. Tools like **Exposed** make accessing databases easier.

Configuring Exposed

Add dependencies for Exposed and a database driver (example: PostgreSQL).

kotlin

```
dependencies {
    implementation("org.jetbrains.exposed:exposed-core:0.37.3")
    implementation("org.jetbrains.exposed:exposed-dao:0.37.3")
    implementation("org.jetbrains.exposed:exposed-
```

```
jdbc:0.37.3")
    implementation("org.postgresql:postgresql:42.3.3")
}
```

Configure the database connection.

kotlin

```
import org.jetbrains.exposed.sql.Database

fun connectDatabase() {
    Database.connect(
        url = "jdbc:postgresql://localhost:5432/mydb",
        driver = "org.postgresql.Driver",
        user = "user",
        password = "password"
    )
}
```

Creating Tables

Use the Exposed DSL to define tables.

kotlin

```
import org.jetbrains.exposed.sql.Table

object Users : Table() {
    val id = integer("id").autoIncrement()
    val name = varchar("name", 50)
    val email = varchar("email", 100)
    override val primaryKey = PrimaryKey(id)
}
```

CRUD Operations

Perform operations on the database.

kotlin

```
import org.jetbrains.exposed.sql.*
```

```kotlin
import org.jetbrains.exposed.sql.transactions.transaction

fun createUser(name: String, email: String) {
    transaction {
        Users.insert {
            it[Users.name] = name
            it[Users.email] = email
        }
    }
}

fun fetchUsers(): List<ResultRow> {
    return transaction {
        Users.selectAll().toList()
    }
}
```

These functions perform insertions and queries in the database.

Integration with Routes

Integrate database operations with Ktor routes.

kotlin

```kotlin
routing {
    post("/users") {
        val params = call.receive<Map<String, String>>()
        createUser(params["name"] ?: "", params["email"] ?: "")
        call.respondText("User created")
    }

    get("/users") {
        val users = fetchUsers().map {
            "${it[Users.name]} (${it[Users.email]})"
        }
        call.respond(users)
    }
}
```

Backend development with Ktor is flexible and powerful, allowing the creation of robust APIs with efficient database integration and secure authentication. Following good modularization, authentication and data management practices ensures reliable and scalable systems.

CHAPTER 22: DEPENDENCY MANAGEMENT

Managing dependencies efficiently is essential for developing robust and scalable projects. Gradle, a powerful and flexible build automation tool, is widely used to manage dependencies in Kotlin projects. This chapter covers using Gradle with Kotlin, how to configure and manage libraries, and offers tips for optimizing the build process.

Uso do Gradle com Kotlin

Gradle is an automation tool that uses configuration files to manage builds, dependencies, and tasks. It supports two main types of DSLs (Domain-Specific Language): **Groovy** and **Kotlin**. Using Gradle Kotlin DSL provides advantages such as autocomplete in the IDE and greater type safety.

Basic Structure of a Gradle File

In Gradle Kotlin DSL, configuration files are written in Kotlin and have the extension .gradle.kts.

kotlin

```
plugins {
    kotlin("jvm") version "1.8.0"
    application
}

group = "com.example"
version = "1.0.0"

repositories {
    mavenCentral()
}
```

```
dependencies {
    implementation(kotlin("stdlib"))
    testImplementation("org.junit.jupiter:junit-jupiter:5.8.2")
}

application {
    mainClass.set("com.example.MainKt")
}
```

Main Components

- **plugins**: Defines the plugins used in the project, such as Kotlin support or Java applications.
- **repositories**: Specifies where dependencies will be downloaded from, such as Maven Central or JCenter.
- **dependencies**: Declares the libraries required for the project.
- **application**: Configures the main class for projects that generate executables.

Running Tasks in Gradle

To run Gradle tasks, use the commands in the terminal:

Compile the project:
bash

```
./gradlew build
```

Run the application:
bash

```
./gradlew run
```

Clean up build artifacts:
bash

```
./gradlew clean
```

Multimodule Configuration

Large projects are often divided into multiple modules to improve code organization and reuse.

Folder Structure

plaintext

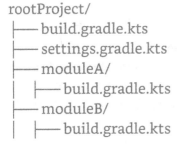

```
rootProject/
├── build.gradle.kts
├── settings.gradle.kts
├── moduleA/
│   ├── build.gradle.kts
├── moduleB/
│   ├── build.gradle.kts
```

File settings.gradle.kts

The file settings.gradle.kts lists the project modules.

kotlin

```
rootProject.name = "MultiModuleProject"

include("moduleA", "moduleB")
```

Dependencies between Modules

Add a dependency from one module to another in the build.gradle.kts.

kotlin

```
dependencies {
    implementation(project(":moduleA"))
}
```

This allows moduleB use the classes and resources defined in moduleA.

Library Configuration and Management

Declaring Dependencies

Dependencies can be added in the sections dependencies. There are different types of dependencies:

- **implementation**: Available only at compile time.
- **api**: Exposed to other modules that depend on this one.
- **testImplementation**: Used only in tests.

kotlin

```kotlin
dependencies {
    implementation("org.jetbrains.kotlin:kotlin-stdlib:1.8.0")
    api("com.google.guava:guava:31.1-jre")
    testImplementation("org.junit.jupiter:junit-jupiter:5.8.2")
}
```

Managing Releases with Release Catalogs

Release catalogs help you centralize and manage dependencies across projects.

Creating a Catalog File

Add a file libs.versions.toml in gradle/.

toml

```toml
[versions]
kotlin = "1.8.0"
junit = "5.8.2"

[libraries]
kotlin-stdlib = { module = "org.jetbrains.kotlin:kotlin-stdlib",
version.ref = "kotlin" }
junit-jupiter = { module = "org.junit.jupiter:junit-jupiter",
```

```
version.ref = "junit" }
```

Using the Catalog

No build.gradle.kts, import the catalog dependencies.

kotlin

```
dependencies {
   implementation(libs.kotlin.stdlib)
   testImplementation(libs.junit.jupiter)
}
```

Configuring Repositories

Repositories define where dependencies will be downloaded from.

kotlin

```
repositories {
   mavenCentral()
   google()
}
```

Popular repositories include:

- **Maven Central**: Standard repository for Java and Kotlin projects.
- **JCenter**: Legacy repository, currently being deprecated.
- **Google**: Required for Android-specific dependencies.

Deleting Transitive Dependencies

Delete unwanted transitive dependencies to avoid conflicts.

kotlin

```
dependencies {
   implementation("org.example:library:1.0") {
      exclude(group = "org.unwanted", module = "unwanted-
```

```
library")
    }
}
```

Tips for Optimizing the Build Process

Parallelism in Build

Enable parallelism to improve performance.

bash

```
./gradlew build --parallel
```

This option allows independent tasks to run simultaneously.

Incremental Build Configuration

Gradle uses incremental build to recompile only what has changed, reducing execution time.

Ensure that your configuration supports this functionality:

kotlin

```
tasks.withType<JavaCompile> {
    options.isIncremental = true
}
```

Build Cache

The build cache stores reusable artifacts to speed up future builds.

Enable caching globally:

bash

```
./gradlew build --build-cache
```

Or configure in the file gradle.properties:

properties

org.gradle.caching=true

Custom Task Configuration

Create custom tasks to automate specific processes.

kotlin

```kotlin
tasks.register("generateReport") {
    doLast {
        println("Generating report...")
        // Code to generate the report
    }
}
```

Run the task with:

bash

```bash
./gradlew generateReport
```

Managing Dependency Versions

Use plugins like **Gradle Versions Plugin** to check for dependency updates.

Add the plugin to the file build.gradle.kts.

kotlin

```kotlin
plugins {
    id("com.github.ben-manes.versions") version "0.42.0"
}
```

List outdated dependencies:

bash

```bash
./gradlew dependencyUpdates
```

Optimizing Packaging

For projects that generate JARs, configure packaging to include only essential dependencies.

kotlin

```
tasks.jar {
    duplicatesStrategy = DuplicatesStrategy.EXCLUDE
    from(configurations.runtimeClasspath.get().map { if
(it.isDirectory) it else zipTree(it) })
}
```

Monitoring Performance

Use o buildScan to analyze build performance.

bash

```
./gradlew build --scan
```

The tool provides insights into bottlenecks and possible improvements.

Good Practices in Dependency Management

1. **Centralize Versions**
   Use version catalogs or global variables to facilitate updates and avoid inconsistencies.
2. **Avoid Unnecessary Dependencies**
   Remove unused libraries to reduce build size.
3. **Utilize implementation Whenever possible**
   Prefer implementation instead of api to encapsulate internal dependencies.
4. **Update Dependencies Regularly**
   Monitor updates to keep the project secure and compatible with new features.
5. **Organize the Build into Multiple Modules**
   Modularize large projects to improve build time and maintainability.
6. **Automate Frequent Tasks**

Create custom tasks to efficiently build, test, and package your project.

Managing dependencies with Gradle in Kotlin gives you full control over the build process and project organization. Adopting efficient configuration, updating and optimization practices ensures that the development cycle is more agile, scalable and sustainable. With the tools and techniques presented, you can build robust and well-structured projects.

CHAPTER 23: GOOD PRACTICES AND CODE STANDARDS

Writing clean, readable code is an essential skill for developers, regardless of the language used. In Kotlin, good code practices and patterns not only improve software quality but also make work more efficient and collaborative. This chapter covers how to write clean code, adopt community-recommended conventions, and refactor projects to make them more optimized and easier to maintain.

Writing Clean and Readable Code in Kotlin

Clean Code Principles

1. **Clarity and Simplicity**
   The code should be easy to understand, even for someone who didn't write it. Avoid unnecessary complex logic.
2. **Meaningful Names**
   Choose descriptive names for variables, functions, and classes.

kotlin

```
// Avoid:
fun calc(x: Int, y: Int): Int = x + y

// Prefer:
fun calculateSum(firstNumber: Int, secondNumber: Int): Int =
firstNumber + secondNumber
```

3. **Short and Focused Functions**
   Each function must perform only one task. Long,

cross-functional roles are difficult to maintain.

kotlin

```kotlin
fun calculateTotalPrice(prices: List<Double>, discount: Double):
Double {
    val subtotal = prices.sum()
    return subtotal - (subtotal * discount)
}
```

4. **Avoid Duplicate Code**
   Use reusable functions to avoid redundancy.

kotlin

```kotlin
fun formatCurrency(value: Double): String = "$
%.2f".format(value)
```

This function can be used whenever it is necessary to format monetary values.

Kotlin Idiomatic Structures

Take advantage of language features to write more idiomatic code.

when **instead of multiple** if-else

kotlin

```kotlin
val day = "Monday"

val typeOfDay = when (day) {
    "Monday", "Tuesday", "Wednesday", "Thursday", "Friday" ->
"Weekday"
    "Saturday", "Sunday" -> "Weekend"
    else -> "Invalid day"
}
```

Scope Functions

Use let, apply, run, also and with to improve readability.

kotlin

```kotlin
val person = Person().apply {
    name = "John Doe"
    age = 30
}
```

Default Values in Parameters

Avoid overloading functions when using default values.

kotlin

```kotlin
fun greet(name: String, greeting: String = "Hello") {
    println("$greeting, $name!")
}
```

Null-Safe Operators

Kotlin offers tools to deal with null safely.

kotlin

```kotlin
val length = nullableString?.length ?: 0
```

Community Recommended Conventions and Standards

Naming Conventions

Classes e Interfaces: Use PascalCase.
kotlin

```kotlin
class UserProfile
```

Variables and Functions: Use camelCase.
kotlin

```kotlin
val userName = "John"
fun calculateTotal()
```

Constants: Use UPPER_SNAKE_CASE.
kotlin

```kotlin
const val MAX_USERS = 100
```

Code Organization
File and Package Structure

Organize code into feature-based packages.

plaintext

```plaintext
com.example.project/
├── ui/
├── data/
├── domain/
```

Order in Kotlin Files

- First the statements import.
- Then classes, functions and properties.

Documentation

Add clear, helpful comments to explain the purpose of the code.

kotlin

```kotlin
/**
 * Calculates the total price after applying a discount.
 *
 * @param prices List of individual item prices.
 * @param discount Percentage discount to apply.
 * @return Total price after discount.
 */
fun calculateTotalPrice(prices: List<Double>, discount: Double):
Double {
```

```
val subtotal = prices.sum()
return subtotal - (subtotal * discount)
}
```

Automated Tests

Write clear and specific tests. Use descriptive names for test methods.

kotlin

```
@Test
fun `should calculate total price with discount`() {
    val prices = listOf(100.0, 50.0)
    val discount = 0.1
    val result = calculateTotalPrice(prices, discount)
    assertEquals(135.0, result)
}
```

Formatting

Use tools like **Kotlin Formatter** or **ktlint** to ensure consistent formatting.

Basic Rules

- Indent with 4 spaces.
- Limit lines to 100 characters if possible.
- Avoid extra blank lines.

Kotlin Project Refactoring and Optimization

Identifying Code That Needs Refactoring

1. **Hard to Read Code**
   If the code requires excessive effort to understand, consider refactoring it.
2. **Duplicate Code**
   Reorganize functions to reuse repeated logic.
3. **Long Functions**

Break long functions into smaller, more specific functions.

Refactoring Tools

- **I understand the idea**: Provides robust support for refactoring such as renaming, extracting methods, and moving classes.
- **SonarQube**: Analyzes code to identify quality issues.

Refactoring Example

Original Code

kotlin

```kotlin
fun calculatePrice(quantity: Int, price: Double): Double {
    val total = quantity * price
    val discount = if (quantity > 10) total * 0.1 else 0.0
    return total - discount
}
```

Refactored Code

kotlin

```kotlin
fun calculatePrice(quantity: Int, price: Double): Double {
    val total = quantity * price
    val discount = calculateDiscount(quantity, total)
    return total - discount
}

private fun calculateDiscount(quantity: Int, total: Double): Double {
    return if (quantity > 10) total * 0.1 else 0.0
}
```

Refactoring improves readability by extracting the discount logic into a separate function.

Kotlin Code Optimization

Avoid Unnecessary Operations

Use collection-specific methods to improve efficiency.

kotlin

```
// Avoid:
val evenNumbers = list.filter { it % 2 == 0 }.map { it * 2 }
```

```
// Prefer:
val evenNumbers = list.asSequence().filter { it % 2 == 0 }.map { it
* 2 }.toList()
```

Use Objetos Singleton

When a class does not need multiple instances, declare it as object.

kotlin

```
object Configuration {
    val baseUrl = "https://api.example.com"
}
```

Avoid Unnecessary Exceptions

Validate data before using it.

kotlin

```
fun divide(a: Int, b: Int): Int {
    require(b != 0) { "Denominator must not be zero" }
    return a / b
}
```

Good Architectural Practices

Follow the SOLID Principle

- **Single Responsibility Principle**: Each class should have only one responsibility.

- **Open/Closed Principle**: Classes must be open for extension, but closed for modification.
- **Liskov Substitution Principle**: Derived classes must be able to replace base classes without problems.
- **Interface Segregation Principle**: Large interfaces should be divided into smaller ones.
- **Dependency Inversion Principle**: Depend on abstractions, not implementations.

Apply Design Patterns

Use appropriate design patterns to solve common problems.

Singleton Pattern

kotlin

```kotlin
object DatabaseConnection {
    fun connect() {
        println("Connected to database")
    }
}
```

Factory Standard

kotlin

```kotlin
class ShapeFactory {
    companion object {
        fun createShape(type: String): Shape {
            return when (type) {
                "circle" -> Circle()
                "square" -> Square()
                else -> throw IllegalArgumentException("Invalid
shape type")
            }
        }
    }
}
```

Repository Pattern

kotlin

```kotlin
interface UserRepository {
    fun getUserById(id: Int): User
}

class UserRepositoryImpl : UserRepository {
    override fun getUserById(id: Int): User {
        // Database query
        return User(id, "John Doe")
    }
}
```

Adopting good code practices and standards in Kotlin not only improves software quality, but also promotes effective collaboration in teams and makes long-term project maintenance easier. By following the guidelines presented, you can write clean, efficient, and scalable code that aligns with the expectations of the Kotlin community.

CHAPTER 24: PUBLISHING KOTLIN PROJECTS

Publishing Kotlin projects and libraries is a fundamental step for developers who want to share their work with the community or distribute it for production use. This chapter covers how to prepare your code for publishing, set up Maven and JCenter repositories, and explore strategies for sharing Kotlin libraries efficiently.

Preparing Your Code for Publishing

Before publishing, it is essential to ensure that the code is clean, functional, and properly documented.

Quality Check

1. **Automated Tests**
   Make sure your project has adequate test coverage. Include unit tests, integration tests and, if applicable, end-to-end tests.

kotlin

```kotlin
@Test
fun `should return correct result`() {
    val result = calculateSum(5, 10)
    assertEquals(15, result)
}
```

2. **Code Analysis**
   Use tools like **ktlint** and **Detekt** to ensure that code follows consistent standards.

Add the **ktlint** in your build.gradle.kts:

kotlin

```
plugins {
    id("org.jlleitschuh.gradle.ktlint") version "10.2.0"
}
```

Run the formatting check:

bash

```
./gradlew ktlintCheck
```

3. **Documentation**
   Include clear comments in your classes and functions
   using the KDoc format.

kotlin

```
/**
* Calculates the sum of two numbers.
*
* @param a First number.
* @param b Second number.
* @return Sum of a and b.
*/
fun calculateSum(a: Int, b: Int): Int = a + b
```

4. **License**
   Add a license to the project to specify terms of use. For
   example, an MIT license:

Create a file LICENSE in the root directory:

plaintext

```
MY License
...
```

Build Configuration

Configure Gradle to generate artifacts suitable for publishing.

Adding Metadata

No build.gradle.kts, include basic information about the project:

kotlin

```
group = "com.example"
version = "1.0.0"

publishing {
    publications {
        create<MavenPublication>("mavenJava") {
            from(components["java"])
            groupId = "com.example"
            artifactId = "my-library"
            version = "1.0.0"
        }
    }
}
```

Generating Artifacts

Include the generation of JAR and Javadoc files:

kotlin

```
tasks.jar {
    manifest {
        attributes["Implementation-Title"] = "My Library"
        attributes["Implementation-Version"] = version
    }
}
```

Create a file sources JAR to include the source code:

kotlin

```
tasks.register<Jar>("sourcesJar") {
```

```
    archiveClassifier.set("sources")
    from(sourceSets.main.get().allSource)
}
```

Add the file sourcesJar to the publication process:

kotlin

```
publishing {
    publications {
        create<MavenPublication>("mavenJava") {
            artifact(tasks["sourcesJar"])
        }
    }
}
```

Working with Maven and JCenter Repositories

Maven and JCenter repositories are the most used for sharing libraries. Although JCenter has been deprecated, Maven Central remains a default choice.

Publishing in Maven Central

1. **Account Creation on Sonatype**
   Register with Sonatype Jira to gain access to Nexus Repository Manager.
2. **Gradle Configuration**
   Configure Gradle to publish to Maven Central:

Add credentials to the file gradle.properties:

properties

```
sonatypeUsername=yourUsername
sonatypePassword=yourPassword
```

No build.gradle.kts, configure the publishing repository:

kotlin

```
publishing {
   repositories {
      maven {
         name = "sonatype"
         url = uri("https://oss.sonatype.org/service/local/
staging/deploy/maven2/")
         credentials {
            username =
project.findProperty("sonatypeUsername") as String?
            password =
project.findProperty("sonatypePassword") as String?
         }
      }
   }
}
```

3. **Artifact Signing**
   Maven Central requires artifacts to be digitally signed.

Add the subscription plugin:

kotlin

```
plugins {
   id("signing")
}

signing {
   sign(publishing.publications)
}
```

Include credentials in the file gradle.properties:

properties

```
signing.keyId=yourKeyId
signing.password=yourPassword
signing.secretKeyRingFile=/path/to/your/secring.gpg
```

Run the publish task:

bash

```
./gradlew publish
```

Strategies for Sharing Kotlin Libraries with the World

Documentation and Examples

1. **README file**
   Include a file README.md with detailed instructions on how to use your library.

markdown

```
# My Library

My Library is a Kotlin library for XYZ functionality.

## Installation

Add the following to your build.gradle.kts:

```kotlin
implementation("com.example:my-library:1.0.0")
```

Usage

kotlin

```kotlin
val result = MyLibrary.doSomething()
println(result)
```

bash

2. **Documentation Site**
   Use tools like **Dokka** to generate HTML documentation.

Add Dokka to the project:

```kotlin

```
plugins {
    id("org.jetbrains.dokka") version "1.6.0"
}

tasks.dokkaHtml {
    outputDirectory.set(buildDir.resolve("dokka"))
}
```

Generate documentation:

bash

```
./gradlew dokkaHtml
```

Promotion and Distribution

1. **GitHub e GitLab**
   Publish your project on open source platforms like GitHub or GitLab for easy access.
2. **NPM Packages (JavaScript)**
   If the library supports Kotlin/JS, publish it to NPM.

Configure o plugin:

kotlin

```
plugins {
    kotlin("js") version "1.8.0"
}

kotlin {
    js {
        browser()
        binaries.executable()
    }
}
```

Add the package to NPM:

bash

```
./gradlew publishJsPackageToNpm
```

3. **Community Outreach**
   Share your project on forums, social networks and specialized groups like Kotlin Slack.

Tips for Publishing Success

1. **Keep the Code Updated**
   Regularly update your library to keep up with changes to Kotlin and dependencies.
2. **Adopt Semantic Versioning**
   Use the pattern **MAJOR.MINOR.PATCH** to manage versions clearly.

plaintext

```
1.0.0 - First stable version.
1.1.0 - Addition of new features.
1.1.1 - Bug fixes.
```

3. **Provide Support and Feedback**
   Respond to user questions and be open to contributions.
4. **Testing and Continuous Integration**
   Use CI/CD to ensure that code changes don't break functionality.

CI configuration example in GitHub Actions:

yaml

```
name: CI

on:
  push:
    branches:
      - main
```

```
jobs:
  build:
    runs-on: ubuntu-latest
    steps:
      - uses: actions/checkout@v2
      - uses: actions/setup-java@v2
        with:
          distribution: 'zulu'
          java-version: '17'
      - uses: actions/setup-gradle@v2
      - run: ./gradlew build
```

Publishing Kotlin libraries is a valuable opportunity to contribute to the community and gain visibility in the development ecosystem. Following best practices for code quality, publishing setup, and promotion ensures your project has impact and is widely adopted.

CHAPTER 25: EXPLORING THE FUTURE WITH KOTLIN

Kotlin has evolved rapidly since its introduction by JetBrains, consolidating itself as a modern, safe and productive language. This chapter explores the future of language, its emerging trends, and how developers can continue to hone their skills to stay current in an ever-changing technology landscape.

The Future of Language and New Trends

Kotlin Multiplatform Expansion

Kotlin Multiplatform (KMP) continues to mature, allowing developers to share code across different platforms such as Android, iOS, backend, and web. With growing support from the community and companies, KMP is becoming a reliable solution for cross-platform projects.

Kotlin Multiplatform's modular architecture allows developers to use common code for business logic while maintaining platform-specific implementations. For example, cross-platform libraries like Kotlinx.serialization and Which already demonstrate how Kotlin can be used to create scalable and efficient applications.

In the future, tools like Compose Multiplatform are expected to gain more prominence, making it easier to create native graphical interfaces across multiple platforms using a single code base.

kotlin

```
// Code shared in KMP
expect fun getPlatformName(): String
```

```
actual fun getPlatformName(): String = "Android"
// For iOS:
actual fun getPlatformName(): String = "iOS"
```

Adapting to New Versions of Kotlin

With each new version, Kotlin introduces performance improvements, new features, and tighter integration with tools and frameworks. Some trends include:

1. **Improved immutability**: Greater focus on immutable data structures to reduce errors and make code more predictable.
2. **Functional programming**: Expanded support for concepts such as monads and currying, which can be adopted through libraries or directly into the language in the future.
3. **Kotlin/Wasm**: With the advancement of WebAssembly (Wasm), Kotlin is already being adapted to generate executable code directly in browsers.

kotlin

```
// Example of function with currying
fun add(a: Int): (Int) -> Int = { b -> a + b }
val addFive = add(5)
println(addFive(10)) // Displays 15
```

Kotlin no Backend e Microsserviços

With the growth of Ktor and integration with tools like Exposed for databases, Kotlin is becoming a strong choice for backend development. Technologies such as GraalVM allow the creation of lighter and faster applications, using Kotlin in optimized environments.

The adoption of Kotlin by large companies on the backend, such as Netflix and Pinterest, demonstrates its viability for high-scale critical solutions.

kotlin

```
// Basic route configuration in Ktor
routing {
    get("/greet") {
        call.respondText("Hello, World!")
    }
}
```

Support for Artificial Intelligence and Machine Learning

Combining Kotlin with frameworks like KotlinDL (Kotlin Deep Learning) and TensorFlow for Kotlin expands your possibilities in the field of artificial intelligence. Clear syntax and coroutine support make Kotlin a suitable language for machine learning experiments and production.

kotlin

```
// Uso básico do KotlinDL
val model = Sequential.of(
    Input(28, 28, 1),
    Conv2D(32, KernelSize(3, 3), activation = Activations.Relu),
    MaxPool2D(poolSize = PoolSize(2, 2)),
    Flatten(),
    Dense(10, activation = Activations.Softmax)
)
```

Emerging Technologies Supported by Kotlin

WebAssembly (Wasm)

WebAssembly is revolutionizing web development, allowing languages like Kotlin to run directly in the browser with near-native performance. Kotlin support for Wasm is still under development, but promises to expand the possibilities for using the language on the web frontend.

Compose Multiplatform

Compose Multiplatform, an extension to Jetpack Compose, lets you create modern, responsive GUIs for Android, desktop, and web with a single code base.

kotlin

```
@Composable
fun Greeting(name: String) {
    Text("Hello, $name!")
}
```

Compose simplifies the development of dynamic interfaces, promoting greater code reuse across platforms.

Integration with Blockchain

Kotlin is being used to develop blockchain-based solutions due to its clean syntax, interoperability with Java, and robust libraries like Web3j, which facilitates access to smart contracts on Ethereum networks.

kotlin

```
// Basic usage example with Web3j
val web3j = Web3j.build(HttpService("https://
mainnet.infura.io/v3/YOUR-PROJECT-ID"))
val ethBalance = web3j.ethGetBalance("YOUR-ADDRESS",
DefaultBlockParameterName.LATEST).send()
println("Balance: ${ethBalance.balance}")
```

Internet of Things (IoT)

With Kotlin Native support, it is possible to develop applications for IoT devices. Kotlin can be used to create software that controls embedded devices or collects data from sensors.

kotlin

```
fun readSensorData(): String {
    // Simulates a sensor reading
    return "Temperature: 22.5°C"
}
```

How to Continue Learning and Evolving Your Skills

Diving Deeper into the Kotlin Ecosystem

1. **Exploration of Official Libraries**
   Explore libraries like Kotlinx.coroutines, Serialization, and Multiplatform to maximize the use of the language's idiomatic features.
2. **Participation in Open Source Projects**
   Contributing to open source projects on GitHub is a great way to learn and gain hands-on experience.

Certifications and Advanced Courses

Earning certifications and completing specialized courses can strengthen your credentials as a Kotlin developer. Platforms like JetBrains Academy, Udemy and Coursera offer high-quality courses.

Communities and Conferences

Join conferences like KotlinConf and user groups on Slack, Reddit, and forums. Being active in the community helps you exchange ideas, learn new practices, and explore emerging trends.

Constant Practices

1. **Write Code Every Day**
   Practicing regularly improves skills and strengthens understanding of concepts.
2. **Build Real World Projects**
   Developing practical applications to solve real-world problems reinforces learning and creates a portfolio

for future opportunities.

kotlin

```
// Simple application to calculate BMI
fun calculateBMI(weight: Double, height: Double): Double =
weight / (height * height)
```

```
val bmi = calculateBMI(70.0, 1.75)
println("Your BMI is: $bmi")
```

The future of Kotlin is bright, with technological advancements and a growing ecosystem of tools and communities. Developers can expand their skills by exploring new areas, such as cross-platform, artificial intelligence, and blockchain, as well as continuing to practice, learn, and contribute to the community. Mastering Kotlin is not only an investment in knowledge, but also a step towards becoming a highly valued technology professional.

FINAL CONCLUSION

Learning Kotlin, explored in depth throughout this book, took us on a technical and practical journey through its features, use cases, and potential. This conclusion serves to summarize the most valuable lessons from each chapter, highlight the impact of mastering Kotlin on a developer's career, and offer a brief thank you to readers for embarking on this journey.

Summary of Key Lessons Learned

Chapter 1: Introduction to Kotlin

The first chapter presented the history and evolution of Kotlin, highlighting why it was created and its advantages over other languages. We learned how interoperability with Java, nullability safety, and a modern syntax make Kotlin a powerful choice. Additionally, we explore the main ecosystems in which Kotlin is applied: Android, backend and cross-platform.

Chapter 2: Configuring the Development Environment

Setting up an efficient environment is the starting point for any project. This chapter detailed how to install IntelliJ IDEA and Android Studio, set up Kotlin projects, and integrate additional tools to increase productivity. With this, we establish a solid foundation to develop fluidly.

Chapter 3: Basic Syntax and Program Structure

By covering the fundamentals, we understand how to declare variables with our and val, work with data types and use type inference. Additionally, we learned the basic structure of a Kotlin program, which combines simplicity and flexibility, allowing new developers to adopt the language quickly.

Chapter 4: Flow Control

Mastery of flow control is essential for solving logic problems. We learn how to use if, else, when and repetition structures like for and while. We discovered how Kotlin allows for idiomatic expressions, such as using when to replace strings of conditionals.

Chapter 5: Roles and Scopes

This chapter explored functions, one of the main pillars of language. We learned how to declare functions, work with default-valued parameters, and use high-order functions, lambdas, and inline functions to write modular, reusable code. Scope was also covered, with an emphasis on using scope functions such as let, apply and run.

Chapter 6: Working with Collections

Collections are fundamental for manipulating data in any application. We study lists, sets and maps, learning to perform operations such as filtering, mapping and grouping. Additionally, we saw how to use sequences to process large volumes of data efficiently.

Chapter 7: Classes and Objects

Object orientation is a central concept in Kotlin. We learned how to declare classes, create objects and use primary and secondary constructors. Properties and methods were discussed as essential elements for structuring object-based programs.

Chapter 8: Inheritance and Polymorphism

Inheritance and polymorphism are essential for code reuse and flexibility in object-oriented programming. This chapter highlighted the use of the modifier open for inheritance, overriding methods and the creation of derived classes, demonstrating how polymorphism facilitates the adaptation of behaviors.

Chapter 9: Interfaces and Abstract Classes

The differentiation between interfaces and abstract classes was explored in this chapter. We've seen how interfaces define reusable contracts and how abstract classes provide a middle ground between concrete implementation and abstract definition. Good practices were presented to create efficient abstractions.

Chapter 10: Working with Strings

Manipulating strings is a common task in any application. We learned how to use string interpolation, work with multiline strings, and apply useful methods for text processing, such as split and replace.

Chapter 11: File Operations

This chapter covered reading and writing files in Kotlin. We learned how to use streams and buffers to manipulate large files and how to ensure the safety and efficiency of these operations.

Chapter 12: Exception Handling

Error handling is crucial to the robustness of the software. We explore how to identify and handle exceptions using blocks try, catch and finally. We also saw how to create custom exceptions for specific scenarios.

Chapter 13: Object-Oriented Programming

We review the pillars of object-oriented programming: encapsulation, inheritance and polymorphism. We applied these concepts to Kotlin projects and learned how to implement popular design patterns like Singleton and Factory.

Chapter 14: Functional Programming

Functional programming is a powerful paradigm supported by Kotlin. We learned to use functions as first-class objects, work with collections using functional operations, and apply concepts like immutability to write safer code.

Chapter 15: Asynchronous Programming

Asynchronous programming was explored using coroutines. We learned to work with launch, async and await, managing competition efficiently. With this, we gain tools to create responsive and scalable applications.

Chapter 16: Integration with APIs

Consuming REST APIs is an indispensable skill. This chapter covered using Retrofit and Ktor to make HTTP calls, as well as techniques for processing JSON responses. We learn to integrate systems efficiently and safely.

Chapter 17: Data Persistence

Data persistence was explored with SQLite and Room, providing tools for storing information locally. We saw how to configure databases, perform basic queries, and manage migrations.

Chapter 18: Automated Testing

Automated testing guarantees software quality. We studied how to create unit and integration tests using JUnit and MockK, in addition to applying good practices for writing clear and effective tests.

Chapter 19: Working with Kotlin Multiplatform

Kotlin Multiplatform opens up new possibilities by sharing code across platforms like Android, iOS, and backend. We explore how to set up cross-platform projects and integrate code specific to each environment.

Chapter 20: Creating Android Applications with Kotlin

Android development was addressed with emphasis on the lifecycle of activities and fragments, as well as the creation of dynamic user interfaces. This chapter provided the tools to create modern, responsive applications.

Chapter 21: Building Backends with Kotlin

The use of Ktor for backend development has been explored in depth. We learned how to configure routes, implement authentication and manage databases, creating robust and scalable APIs.

Chapter 22: Dependency Management

With Gradle, managing dependencies becomes more efficient. We saw how to configure Kotlin projects, optimize builds and use best practices to keep the development environment clean and functional.

Chapter 23: Good Practices and Code Standards

Writing clean, readable code is a critical skill. We learn to adopt community-recommended conventions, refactor code to improve its structure, and apply popular design patterns.

Chapter 24: Publishing Kotlin Projects

Publishing libraries and projects is an important step towards contributing to the community. This chapter explored how to prepare code for publishing, set up Maven repositories, and strategies for promoting Kotlin libraries.

Chapter 25: Exploring the Future with Kotlin

The future of Kotlin is promising, with advances in cross-platform, artificial intelligence and blockchain. We learn how to continue evolving our skills and exploring new opportunities.

Impact of Mastering Kotlin on your Career and Projects

Mastering Kotlin is not only a technical achievement, but also a competitive differentiator. The language is constantly growing and is widely adopted in various industries. Developers proficient in Kotlin have access to opportunities in areas such as Android development, backend, cross-platform solutions, and even emerging technologies like artificial intelligence and IoT.

Furthermore, the language's clear syntax and advanced features make development more efficient, allowing you to create robust applications with less effort. Well-structured Kotlin projects are easier to maintain and scale, resulting in time and resource savings in the long term.

I sincerely thank you, the reader, for taking the time and energy to explore this manual. We hope the lessons presented here have not only expanded your knowledge, but also sparked your passion for developing with Kotlin. Your commitment to learning is the key to success on your journey as a developer. May this book be a milestone in your professional growth and inspire new projects and achievements.

Greetings,

Diego Rodrigues